Dial-Up And *Daydreams*

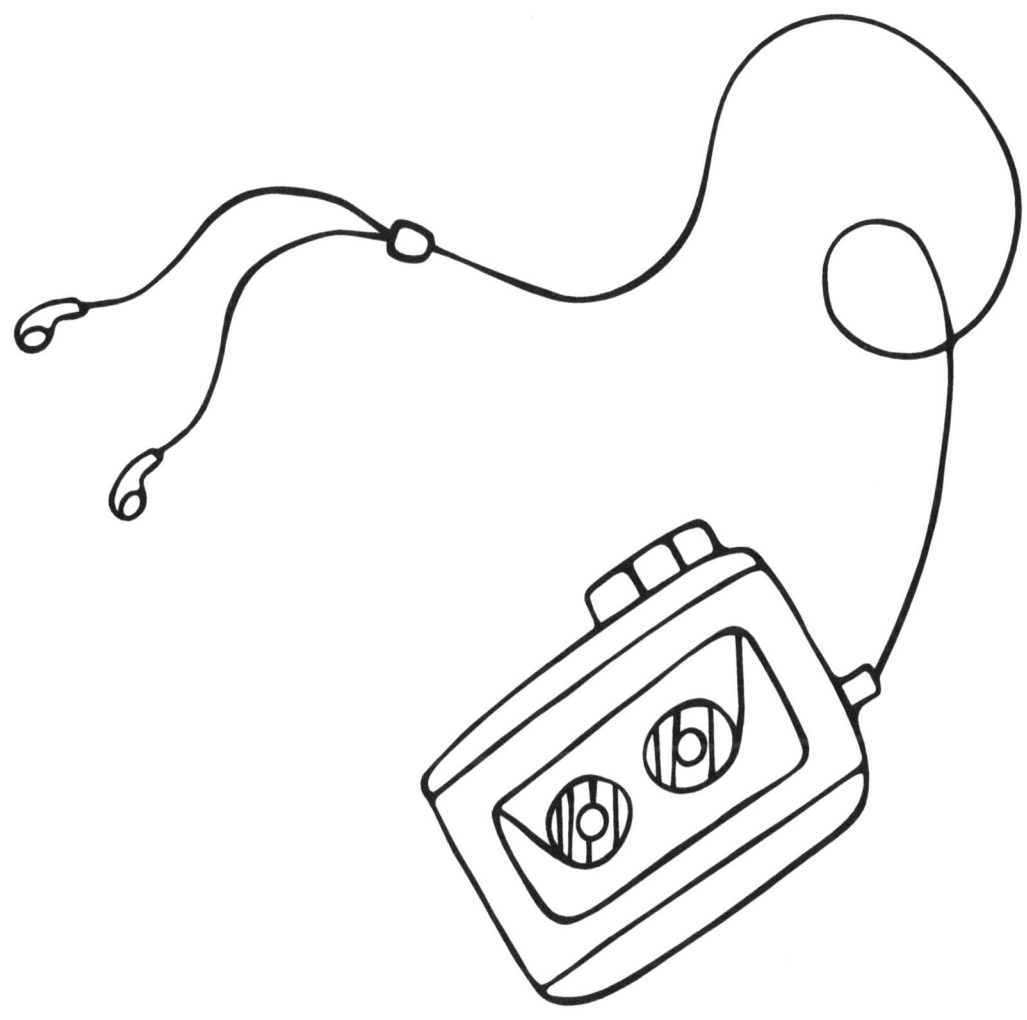

Britt Wolfe

Copyright © 2025 Britt Wolfe

All rights reserved. No part of this anthology may be copied, shared, or slipped into a locker note without the author's written permission. That includes photocopying, recording, or reciting dramatically into the void at 2AM.

This is a work of creative expression. The moments, memories, and mixtape-worthy heartaches within are fictional—or at least lovingly fictionalized. Any resemblance to real people, places, or crushes you never quite got over is purely coincidental. (But let's be honest—you were probably there too.)

All poems, stories, and slow-dialled confessions are the product of the author's imagination, lived experience, and unrelenting obsession with turning feelings into words.

Cover design, formatting, and late-night rewording by Britt Wolfe. Soul-guarding and snack-stealing by Sophie and Lena, who have excellent taste in poetry.

First Edition: 2025
ISBN: 978-1-0695065-1-1

Printed in Canada, where even our nostalgia says sorry.

For questions, permissions, praise, or if you still remember your first MSN screen name, visit: BrittWolfe.com

If this collection made you feel something, please consider leaving a review. If it didn't, maybe come back to it someday. Nostalgia has a funny way of growing up with us.

This anthology is dedicated to:

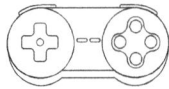 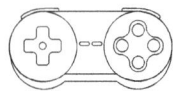 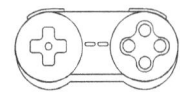 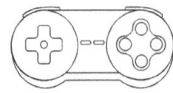 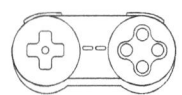

The culture that raised me-

To the songs that played on scratchy speakers and the ones that still echo in my bones.

To the television shows that taught me what friendship, heartbreak, and rebellion looked like.

To the news stories that shaped my understanding of the world, one headline at a time.

To the trends I clung to, laughed at, grew out of, and secretly still love.

You didn't just entertain me.

You shaped me.

And somewhere between the dial tones and the daydreams, I became who I am.

This story is for all of you.

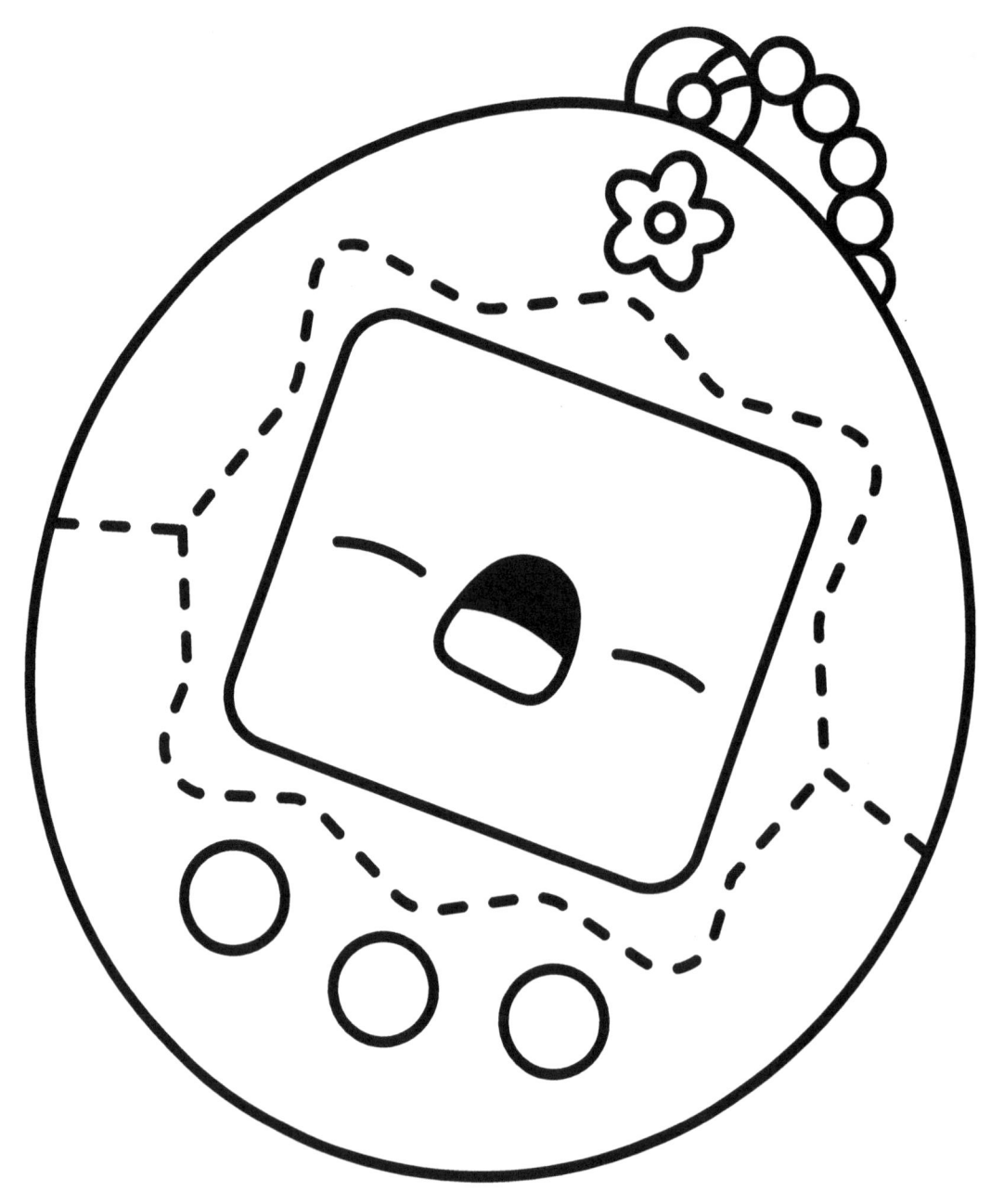

Poems and fragments from a pop culture childhood

This book is a love letter to the versions of us we left behind in old chat logs and notebook margins.

To the girls who stayed up late listening to burned CDs on Discmans that skipped when you walked too fast.

To the boys who wrote bad poetry about unspoken crushes and never showed it to anyone.

To the queer kids who didn't yet have the language, but knew the lyrics that made them feel seen.

To the ones who scrolled fan forums under bedsheets and waited for the sound of dial-up to connect them to somewhere that felt like belonging.

These pages are made of pop culture and paper cuts. Of locker-lined longing and after-school reruns. Of AIM away messages, movie quotes, song lyrics, and the deep, confusing ache of becoming.

It's not a complete record of that time—how could it be? But it's an emotional one.

A scrapbook of feeling. A playlist in poetic form. A tender time capsule.

Some of it is funny. Some of it hurts. Some of it might remind you of a version of yourself you forgot you missed. All of it is real.

So here's to the mixtapes, the slow-danced mistakes, the *Dawson's Creek* dialogues we used to quote like scripture. May these poems find you where you are—and take you back to where you were.

Keep the dial tone soft and your daydreams loud,

Britt Wolfe

Table Of Contents

Forward: Poems and fragments from a pop culture childhood.....05

Act I: Breaking The World Gently.....09

    Introduction: Broadcast In Real Time.....11
    We All Saw It.....14
    When The Music Stopped.....17
    The House Burned Down on TV.....18
    Kurt Cobain Fell Silent.....20
    The White Bronco.....24
    Speaker's Corner Prayers.....27
    Taped Off the News at Nine.....28
    Newspaper Girl.....29
    The Year Everyone Went Online.....30
    Oklahoma City Murmurs.....32
    JonBenét's America.....36
    The Sound of Typing.....39
    Hold the Phone.....40
    The Royal Divorce.....42
    Diana Died.....45
    Death of the Landline.....47
    The Ice Storm of '98.....49
    The Clinton Scandal.....52
    Flipped to Page A6.....55
    The Columbine Bell.....57
    Static on the Line.....61
    Y2K and the Countdown to the Future.....63

Act II: Scheduled Programming.....66

    Introduction: Previously On.....67
    TV Guide Tarot.....68
    Saved by the Bell, Broken by the Rest.....70
    This Is a Story All About How.....73
    Viewer Discretion Advised.....75
    The One Where They Were Everything.....76
    In Syndication.....79
    Sabrina Was My Religion.....81
    Code Blue at Country General.....84
    When Cory Loved Topanga.....87
    The After School Specials.....90
    Black Box Glow.....92
    MuchMusic: Video Killed Nothing.....93
    Be Kind Rewind.....95
    Wishing on a Dawson.....98
    X Philes.....100
    The VHS Tape We Wore Out.....102
    Full House, TGIF.....104
    Let Us Show You Something.....107
    The Buffy Effect.....110
    The Show About Nothing.....113
    Late Night with Nobody.....117
    Tape Over.....118

Table Of Contents Continued

Act III: Hit Replay.....119

    Introduction: Press Play to Feel Everything.....120
    The Seattle Sound.....122
    An Ode to the Rear.....124
    The Voice That Could Break a Century.....126
    The Secret Track.....128
    The Sign.....130
    Creep.....131
    Truth-Tellers in Harmony.....132
    Liner Notes.....134
    The Most Flawless Album Ever Made.....136
    When the Noise Fell Away.....138
    The Band That Took On the Giant.....142
    Blue Smoke.....143
    Don't Go Chasing.....144
    The Australian Invasion.....145
    The Angry Young Women.....148
    Woman Behind the Feedback.....151
    The Flowers Were Dead.....153
    Parklife vs. Champagne Supernova.....155
    When the World Needed Glitter and Grit.....157
    Like Thunder.....159
    Two Voice, One Legacy.....161
    The Velvet Rope.....163
    The First Song I Cried To.....164
    Ahead by a Century.....165
    Lilith Fiar.....167
    The Blueprint was Missy.....170
    Napster.....172
    White boy Ragecore.....174
    Woodstock '99.....177
    The time of Your Life.....179

A Final Reflection: Rewinding Softly.....181

The Pages Between Us: The Poetry And Prose Series.....184

About The Author: Britt Wolfe.....186

Act I:
Breaking The World Gently

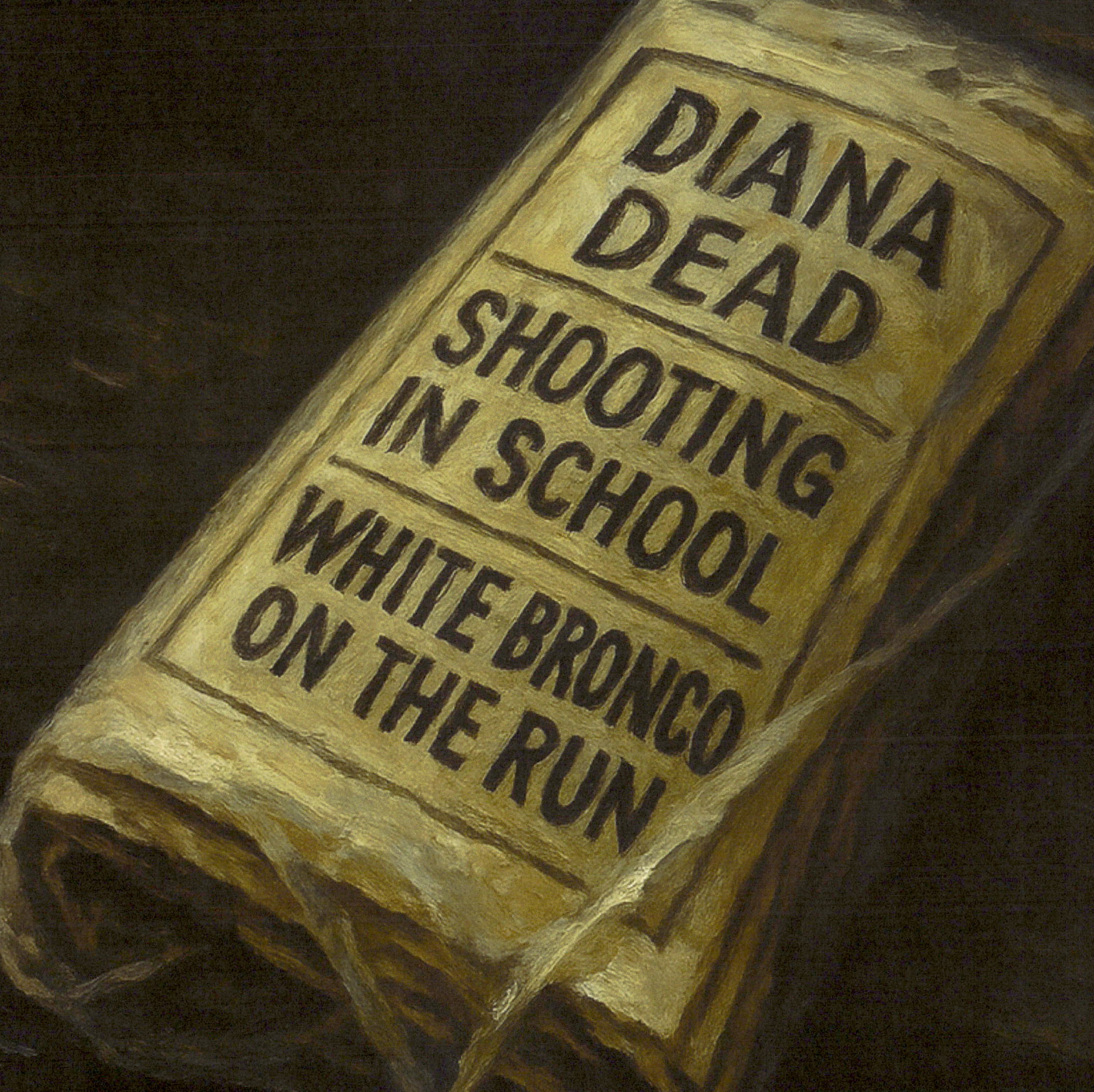

Broadcast in Real Time

We didn't mean to witness the world unravel. We were just trying to watch cartoons.

But the news kept interrupting. A white Bronco sped down a freeway we'd never driven. A school we'd never heard of suddenly became a headline. A princess we didn't know we loved was lost in a flash, her story breaking before we even understood what we were hearing.

The volume was never loud enough to explain, but the images were clearer than they should have been. We sat cross-legged on shag carpet, cradling cereal bowls full of sugary goodness, changing the channel—then changing it back. Because something in us, even then, knew this mattered. Even if we didn't understand why yet.

This was the decade when childhood cracked open. Not with a bang, but with a broadcast. We watched tragedy roll in with the morning paper, heard the tension in our parents' phone calls, and felt the shift in our classrooms when the TV cart appeared and no one smiled. It was all "live." All now. All ours, whether we were ready or not.

And so, we folded the headlines into our growing selves. We wrapped our memories in plastic like the newspaper on the porch and pressed play on whatever came next.

This is what it felt like to come of age in a world that was breaking slowly, gently, right there on Channel 3.

We All Saw It

We all saw it.

Not rumour. Not hearsay.
Not some whispered injustice buried in the back of a newspaper.
It was right there.
In pixelated truth.
Lit by streetlamps.
Framed by disbelief.

Rodney King.
On the ground.
Defenceless.
Human.

And still, they beat him.

Like his body offended them.
Like his survival was the crime.
Like they were trying to beat history into him—
every crack of the baton,
a reminder that Blackness is never safe,
not even when you're down.

We saw his body buckle.
We saw the blood.
We counted the swings—
over fifty.
We flinched with each one.

And still—*they said not guilty.*

The justice system didn't just fail.

It spit in faces.

Told us the camera was lying.
Told us our eyes were wrong.
Told us truth doesn't matter
when it stands on Black skin.

And the city erupted.

Not in chaos.
In clarity.

The smoke wasn't confusion.
It was grief on fire.
It was fury with no exit.
It was what happens when you scream into a country that keeps putting its fingers in its ears.

Rodney King, bruised and broken,
still found the strength to ask,
"Can we all get along?"

And what did we do?
We turned his plea into a punchline.
Played it on late-night.
Mocked the man who had been made into a warning.
The man who offered peace
after the world had offered him hell.

That was 1991.

But the tape never stopped rolling.

Eric.
Tamir.
Sandra.
George.
Tyre.
And a thousand names we'll never hear,
because some cameras weren't turned on in time.

We keep seeing it.
And seeing it.
And seeing it.

And still—it keeps happening.

The world didn't just watch Rodney King.
It studied the footage.

And learned nothing.

BREAKING NEWS
SELENA DEAD AT 23

when the music stopped

she was still smiling
when the headline
appeared.
the screen flickered.
the room went quiet.
someone said,
"not her."

The House Burned Down on TV

I was eating dinner when the fire started.
Mac and cheese, a paper napkin,
the news playing quietly in the other room.

They called it a standoff.
But it looked like a house holding its breath.
Smoke curling like a secret.
Flames licking the sky like they were born hungry.

The anchor's voice didn't shake.
He said "compound" like it was a word
children should already know.

The camera didn't flinch.
It just watched—
while the windows bloomed orange,
and the walls folded in like prayer hands giving up.

Someone muted it.
But the fire kept talking.

I asked if everyone got out.
No one answered.
Someone passed the ketchup.

Later, I learned about cults and tear gas and babies
and how long it takes for a roof to give.
But back then,
it was just another house
that no one tried to save.

A house that burned down on TV
while a whole country watched
and didn't change the channel.

Kurt Cobain Fell Silent

I didn't know who he was when he died.

Not really.

I knew the name—vaguely. Knew he was the one with the ripped jeans and the hair that never quite stayed out of his face. Knew he was the voice behind that band someone older listened to—Nirvana—like it was just noise, a phase, something reckless and loud. No one really noticed what I was listening to. But I understood him. Even though I wasn't supposed to. Even though I wouldn't have told anyone why. Something in his voice made sense to me. Something in the ache of it. The way he sounded like he was breaking and screaming and trying to disappear—all at once.

But when the news came—when the headline hit the television screen and everyone went quiet—something changed. Something in the air. Like the volume had been turned down on the whole world.

Even the sunlight looked different that day.

Someone said, "He killed himself," and someone else whispered, "Of course he did," like it was inevitable. Like some people are born to break.

I didn't understand his music then.
Not really.
But I felt the loss.
God, I felt it.

Felt it in the silence that swallowed the radio between songs.

Felt it in the way no one made eye contact when his voice played again.

Felt it in the pause between the chords of *Come As You Are*, and the endless echo that followed.

We didn't talk about mental health back then. Not at school. Not in church. Not at the dinner table. Not even when it curled up in the back of the classroom, silent and twitching. Not even when it took someone the world loved.

Instead, we turned it down. Or we turned it up too loud to think.

We wore his lyrics like patches on our backpacks. We drew the Nirvana smiley face on our binders and carved it into desks. We copied the words we didn't yet understand and made them our own. "I miss the comfort in being sad," we scribbled, like it explained everything.

Grief echoed through us—soft, then loud.
Louder than we could handle.
And still, we kept playing the CD.

Because it wasn't just about Kurt. It was about what he carried.

The weight of being too much.
The ache of being watched and still not seen.
The terror of being loved for what hurts you most.

And maybe, too, the fear that if someone like him couldn't make it—
someone that brilliant, that loud, that real—
then maybe none of us could.

But we kept listening.

Because in his silence,
something opened.

And we stepped into it, one by one.
Teenagers with stereo hearts and splintered selves,
hoping that somewhere between distortion and chorus,
we'd find a way to survive.

The White Bronco

The pizza was still hot
when the chase began.
Friday night,
mid-June,
and a whole country
changed the channel at once.

On one screen:
the Knicks in Game Five.
On another:
a white blur
on blacktop,
cruising toward disbelief
at thirty-five miles an hour.

America watched itself
watching itself.
Split screen.
Split country.
Split man in the back of a Bronco,
cradling a gun
like a question
no one wanted answered.

Helicopters buzzed like flies
over the freeway.
The news anchor
tried to sound calm.
The crowd on the overpass cheered
like it was a parade.
It wasn't.

We didn't know
what side we were on.
Just that it felt like
we were supposed to choose one.
And still,
the Bronco kept driving.
Slow.
Steady.
White.

History doesn't always crash.
Sometimes
it rolls
softly
through L.A.,
with the windows up
and the world watching.

Speaker's Corner Prayers

We lined up to be heard.
Pressed our faces to the glass
and spilled whatever truth
we could fit in sixty seconds.

No script.
No edits.
Just hope,
and a country that might
be watching.

Taped Off the News at Nine

We taped it—
right off the news at nine.
The war,
the weather,
the words no one knew how to say.

A VCR blinked 12:00
while a man in a tie
told us everything was fine.

Smoke in the distance.
Cuts to commercial.
Back to a map
lit up like a threat.

Our dinner got cold
while they circled a school on the screen.
And the names of the dead
rolled by
like credits.

The tape hissed.
The anchor blinked.
We rewound it.
Watched again.
Paused where the silence felt heaviest.

Some of us learned fear that way.
Some of us learned
nothing at all.

The Newspaper Girl

She was always early.
Pedalling past our window with folded headlines in one hand and a Walkman tucked into her hoodie pocket. She didn't wave. Just nodded sometimes—once, twice, like a secret only we shared.

The papers were always wrapped tight, plastic gleaming with dew. But sometimes —only sometimes—she'd tuck something else inside: a pressed flower, a sticker, a page from a comic folded like origami. Once, a note that said I hope today is better than *yesterday*.

We never knew her name.
But for a few quiet mornings,
she was the only one who remembered we were here.

The Year Everyone Went Online

It didn't happen all at once.

It wasn't fireworks or fanfare or some grand flipping of a switch. It was subtler than that. Like a hum rising in the walls. Like dial tone static stitched into the air. One day we were playing outside until the streetlights came on. The next, we were asking for "just five more minutes" to finish our GeoCities page.

There was something almost holy about it. The way the screen flickered to life. The way the cursor blinked like it was waiting for us to speak. The sound of the modem—groaning, clicking, catching—felt like a door being forced open in another dimension.

We typed like we had something to say. And maybe for the first time, we did.

Message boards. Chat rooms. Anonymous screen names that made us feel a little braver, a little weirder, a little more us. We sent poems to strangers and secrets to best friends and somehow, it all felt safer across the wire.

There were rules, sure. "Don't talk to people you don't know." "Don't give out your real name." But we broke them anyway, because we were hungry—for conversation, for connection, for a world bigger than our bedrooms.

It wasn't just about logging on.
It was about being *found*.

By people who got our references.
By friends who understood our silences.
By feelings we didn't yet have language for, until someone else typed them first.

We didn't know it was a revolution.
Not then.

But the year everyone went online
was the year everything changed.

Oklahoma City Murmurs

No one explained it.
Not properly.

They said there had been an explosion.
A bomb.

Something about a federal building.
Something about daycare.
Something about hate.

But the details came slow, in pieces, like trying to remember a dream while it's still slipping away. The TV showed dust and broken walls and someone crying into a microphone. Someone said the man who did it was American. White. Angry.

That didn't make sense.
We thought we knew what danger looked like.
It didn't look like him.

At school, the teachers turned the volume down.
They used words like tragedy and unthinkable.
They told us to pray.
They told us not to worry.
But the way they said it made us worry more.

The pictures on the news looked like war.
Like something that should have happened somewhere else.
Not in Oklahoma.
Not to kids.
Not in quiet place in the middle of America.

We didn't know what we were supposed to feel.
Just that everything felt off.
Like the walls were thinner.
Like the world could break open anywhere.

So we listened.
To the radio.
To our parents' whispers behind closed doors.
To the murmurs that slipped between headlines and bedtime.

We didn't understand it all.
But we understood enough.
Enough to feel the shift.
Enough to know something sacred had been shattered.
Enough to carry it with us—quietly, always.

JonBenét's America

She was six,
with hair like spun sugar
and a smile rehearsed in the mirror
until it shone brighter than truth.
Cameras loved her.
So did the headlines.
So did a country that didn't know what else to love.

We called it a tragedy—
but only after we called it a mystery.
Only after the documentary deals
and the salacious speculation,
after the neighbours leaned closer,
after the news anchors turned their voices into velvet,
smoothing over the horror
until it sounded like entertainment.

She was six,
but her photos were grown.
Lashes too long, lips too red,
shoulders too bare for a world
this sharp.
We made her older.
Then punished her for it.
We turned her body into a battleground
between innocence and spectacle
and then wondered why it bled.

Blame is America's favourite sport.
Was it the mother?
The pageants?
The ransom note in ransom font?
Was it the brother with his strange silence?
The father with his polished grief?
The home too big to hold the truth?

We devoured her in fragments—
still frames,
evidence bags,
voiceovers
layered over slow pans of suburban snow.

She became America's daughter,
but only after she was gone.
Only after her death became
content.
Only after her name became
a category.
Only after she could no longer speak for herself.

They called her beauty queen,
never child.
They called it a mystery,
never a murder.
They called it a story,
and we listened like it was bedtime,
like it would soothe us.
Like we weren't the ones who wrote the ending
with our teeth.

She was six.
And we still look at her like a mirror.

the sound of typing

it wasn't the news.
it was dana_17.
all caps.
"no way. turn on cnn."

i heard it before i saw it—
that soft staccato,
keys tapping
like a heart skipping.

the truth came
with typos and timestamp.
and just like that,
everything
was different.

hold the phone

caller id
blinked too late—
you were already
on three-way
with her.

The Royal Divorce

It was never just a wedding. It was a spectacle. A promise not just between two people, but between a monarchy and a watching world. They called it a fairytale, and we—hungry for magic—believed them. We watched through television screens and grainy news footage as a young woman became a symbol of something more. A bride. A future queen. The beginning of a story that had already been written for her.

But love—real love—doesn't survive on ceremony.

What we saw in the years that followed wasn't love at all, not the kind we'd been promised. It was duty. It was silence. It was her eyes drifting toward the floor as he spoke over her. It was his hands behind his back during interviews. It was not a look, but the absence of one. Not an argument, but the noise that bloomed in its wake. It was two people trying not to touch, not to flinch, not to break the illusion while the whole world watched.

What we witnessed wasn't a relationship—it was the unraveling of a myth. There were cameras at all the right moments. Flashbulbs catching the split-second expressions they didn't mean to reveal. His boredom. Her sadness. His sharpness. Her restraint. Royalty made their silence golden, but hers rang out louder than any crown could contain. Her smile grew quieter. Her voice more sure. And when she walked through landmines and hospitals and heartbreaks, she did it alone. On camera. In heels.

He looked like history. She looked like rebellion.

And when the divorce came, it was not a bang but a sigh of relief. The end of a performance so long-running it had lost its cast. There was no confetti. No final kiss. Just headlines. Just ink. Just the reminder that even palaces have walls that echo with arguments, that even kingdoms crumble at the altar of unmet expectation.

Love, it turns out, cannot be orchestrated.

And the fairytale?

It was a warning.

Diana Died

It was still dark when the world found out.

Not night, not morning—just that lonely space in between, where time pauses and breath catches. Radios whispered it first, hesitant and stunned. News anchors choked on the shape of her name. Diana. Princess. Gone.

And in homes across continents, people sat up in bed, confused by the quiet. In kitchens, kettles boiled without being poured. In living rooms, televisions flickered like candles. The footage rolled on repeat—Paris streets glazed in rain, the tunnel glowing with cruel finality, the shattered black car. The echo of sirens and the hush of disbelief.

Diana died.

It sounded impossible. Like myth unraveling in real time.

Because she was not supposed to die. Not her. Not the woman who turned monarchy into something mortal. Not the princess who walked through landmines in heels. Not the mother who knelt in pressed trousers to hug children nobody else would touch.

She had become more than royal. She was real.

And in the days that followed, the grief spilled beyond protocol. Bouquets piled high as barricades. A sea of sunflowers and teddy bears and trembling hands pressed to palace gates. Grown men cried openly. Children wrote notes in crayon. Candles lined the streets like prayers with wax wicks.

We mourned her the way we mourned ourselves. Our innocence. Our belief in the fairytale.

Because Diana didn't just wear the crown. She carried the weight of a world that never really forgave her for shining brighter than it.

And yet—she shone anyway.

They told us she'd found peace. But peace should not come in a tunnel. It should not wear seatbelts and flashbulbs and the crush of escape.

Peace should have found her long before we lost her.

But still, somehow, she remains. In the curve of a young prince's jaw. In the scent of fresh hyacinths. In every woman who refuses to be what they expect, and every heart that dares to love loudly and break beautifully.

Diana died.

But her tenderness did not.

death of the landline

she's still there,
curled cord coiled like a memory,
off-white, dusted with the last thing you said.

her dial tone hums—
a ghost in four tones,
flat-lining through the kitchen wall.

no one calls now.
the answering machine blinks
for no one.

she waits anyway,
receiver resting like a prayer
you forgot to finish.

The Ice Storm of '98

It came like sleep—
slow, silver,
settling into the bones of the world.

Streetlights blinked
through frozen lashes.
Trees bowed like old women
under the weight of a sky
that forgot how to melt.

Power lines snapped
like brittle nerves.
The silence wasn't silence—
it was the hum of everything
we used to take for granted
vanishing.

We lit candles,
boiled snow,
spoke in whispers
like the storm might hear us.

Children slept in snowsuits,
fathers chopped wood with trembling hands,
mothers rationed hope
like powdered milk.

No school.
No stores.
No sound
but the slow shatter
of ice shedding its weight.

The world had stopped
just enough to remind us—
civilization is a thin, warm lie
and winter
always tells the truth.

The Clinton Scandal

She was twenty-four.
He was the most powerful man on the planet.

That should have been the headline.
Instead, it was jokes about cigars and dry cleaning.

We turned a woman into a scandal,
a name into a punchline,
a life into collateral damage.

Monica wasn't just young—she was alone.
Intern.
Unpaid.
Working in a house where secrets lined the walls like insulation.
He called her in. She said yes.
And so the world said she asked for it.

What do you call it when a man who signs treaties and orders drone strikes
also unbuckles his belt behind closed doors and calls it private?
We didn't have the words back then.
Or we weren't ready to use them.

So we used hers.
Over and over.
Until she wasn't a person anymore—
just an eye-roll,
a slutty whisper,
a shame we pretended belonged only to her.

We let the man keep his legacy.
We asked the girl to disappear.

And Hillary—oh, Hillary.
They said she stood by him.
But she stood like steel.
The way women do when the whole house is burning
and they're expected to pour the tea.

We hated her for it.
Called her cold.
Unfeeling.
As though loyalty to the knife makes you the one who stabbed it.
As though being cheated on
is somehow more shameful
than doing the cheating.

She was humiliated,
and then blamed for surviving the humiliation.
We acted like the betrayal was hers to answer for—
like his actions wore her face.

It was never just about sex.
It was about power.
And who was allowed to hold it without bleeding for it.

Now we know better.
Now we have words like imbalance and abuse of office and grooming.
Now we ask different questions—
not what did she do,
but why was he allowed?

But knowing better doesn't erase what we did.
We buried a girl alive
and called it democracy.

Flipped to Page A6

It was buried beneath stock reports and weather maps,
beneath the headline everyone was arguing about,
beneath the photograph of a man who looked important.

Just a few lines.
A name you didn't know.
A town you'd never heard of.
A tragedy that didn't scream loud enough to make the front page.

You almost skipped it.
Would've, if your coffee hadn't cooled.
If your thumb hadn't lingered.

But you read it.
And it stayed.
Long after the headlines faded.

Because sometimes the stories that matter most
are the ones we barely see.

The Columbine Bell

There is a bell in Littleton, Colorado, heavy with memory. It hangs in the kind of silence that makes you pause mid-step, unsure whether it's reverence or regret that's pressing on your chest.

It doesn't ring often. But even in its stillness, it tolls.

You can feel it in the way people lower their voices when they speak of April. In the way they glance at the clock when it nears 11:19. In the tightness of a teacher's voice, the sudden hush in a crowded hallway, the security cameras that now decorate every school like uneasy ornaments.

The bell tolls for thirteen.

Thirteen lives taken. Twelve students. One teacher. Names that became vigils. Faces that became headlines. Children whose last moments were spent in confusion, in fear, in places meant to be safe.

But the bell tolls for more than just the murdered.

It tolls for the kids who ran. For the kids who hid. For the kids who played dead beneath desks and the kids who whispered final prayers in closets too small to contain the terror. It tolls for the children who survived with scars invisible to the eye, who still carry the weight of that day in the tension between their shoulders, in the nightmares that return uninvited.

And—uncomfortably, unbearably—it tolls for two more.

Dylan and Eric.

Two boys who were once children too.

Before the supposed trench coats. Before the guns. Before they became symbols, monsters, warnings.

They were babies once. Held. Named. Loved. Not born to kill—but slowly unravelled by something we still don't understand well enough. Hurt boys. Angry boys. Isolated. Dismissed. Lost.

They do not get forgiveness here. This is not absolution.

But they are not left out of the grief.

Because grief, true grief—the kind that echoes through generations—is not selective.

It sees the system that failed them, too. The warning signs missed. The mental health untreated. The boys who fell through every crack until they cracked the world open in return.

The bell mourns them differently. Not as heroes. Not as innocents.

But as part of the tragedy.

Because if we cannot hold space for the whole truth, even the ugly parts, we will never stop this from happening again.

The bell tolls for Rachel and Isaiah. For Lauren and John. For Cassie and Kelly. For Steve and Kyle. For Daniel R, and Corey and Daniel M. and Matthew and William.

And the bell tolls for Dylan and Eric.

And now Anne Marie Hochhalter.

Not to equate.

But to witness.

To name the fullness of the loss.

To admit that a world that creates shooters is a world that must change, not only in response to death—but in prevention of it.

America is loud with bells.

But this one should be listened to differently.

It does not just mourn the slain.

It mourns the boys who became murderers, and the systems that raised them.

It mourns every parent who saw it coming too late.

Every school that looked away.

Every child who wondered if they mattered.

The Columbine bell does not toll to remind us of a moment in history.

It tolls to mark the moment we still haven't learned from.

And beneath its aching chime, there is a plea—that we stop creating children who feel like they have no other way to scream.
That we reach them earlier.
That we see them clearer.
That we build a world where no child, no matter how angry or sad or fractured, ever reaches for a gun before someone reaches for them.

And maybe, someday, the bell will ring for the last time.
And that sound won't be sorrow.

It will be mercy.
It will be change.
It will be peace.

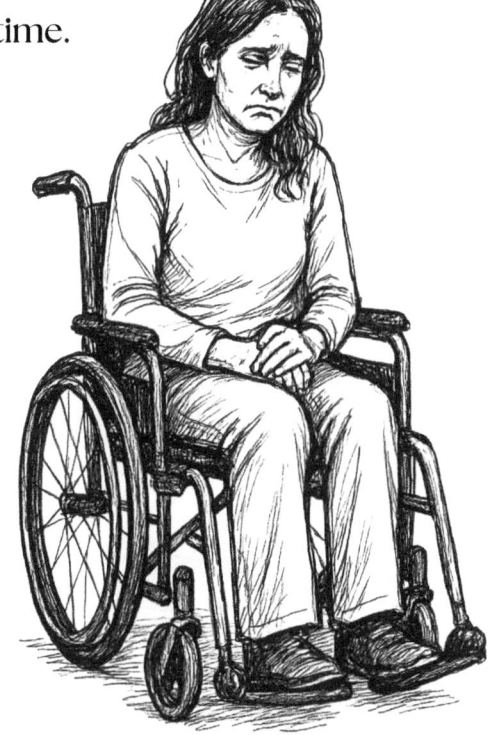

Static on the Line

The screen crackled—static dancing like ghosts between the pixels. A girl ran. Someone screamed. A blur of lockers, a flinch of motion, the soundless violence of a hallway coming undone.

And we watched—paralysed.

Hands over mouths. Tears carving silence.

The horror didn't stay behind the glass.

It came through.

And settled in us, forever.

But nothing changed.

Y2K and the Countdown to the Future

11:50
They said the world might end at midnight.
That the code was broken,
that the clocks we trusted would stumble,
reset to nothing,
forget who we were.

11:51
Banks braced.
Planes hovered.
Families filled bathtubs,
just in case water stopped remembering how to flow.

11:52
And yet—
beneath fluorescent lights and disco balls,
the music kept going.
People danced anyway.
We were born of uncertain nights.

11:53
Floppy disks in drawers.
Modems screeching their mechanical lullabies.
And still, a sense—
that maybe we were hurtling
toward something beautiful.

11:54
The world was getting smaller.
Messages crossed oceans
in the time it took to breathe.
We were connected now.
Wire to wire.
Heart to heart.

11:55
Outside, fireworks stood ready.
Inside, hands held one another.
An entire planet counting together—
One beat.
One hope.
One second at a time.

11:56
Maybe machines would crash.
Maybe they wouldn't.
But we—
we had made it this far.
And that had to mean something.

11:57
In every country,
on every tongue,
the same question floated:
What comes next?

11:58
And maybe it didn't matter.
Because this moment—
this inhale—
was its own kind of miracle.

11:59
So we kissed.
And we screamed.
And we closed our eyes.
Not in fear—
but in reverence.

12:00
Nothing broke.
Everything began.

The Daily News

JANUARY 1, 2000

MILLENNIUM BUG FAILS TO BITE

...ajor problems reported as world marks Y2K

Act II:
Scheduled Programming

Previously On...

This was the golden age of television and the silver glow of comfort.

We gathered around small screens with big hearts, living and reliving every rerun like it mattered. And it did matter. It mattered that Ross said Rachel's name at the altar. That Buffy kept saving the world, again and again. That Cory and Topanga found their way back to each other. It mattered that Will made us laugh before we understood his pain. That a cartoon family on a worn-out couch could somehow feel like our own. That Dawson's Creek made us believe our feelings had depth, even when we didn't have the words for them. And that Saturday mornings weren't just for cereal—they were for wonder.

From sitcoms to teen dramas to animated shows that cracked our hearts open in quiet, unexpected ways, this section is a remote control through memory. Every show was a friend. Every episode, a time capsule.

These poems and prose remember what it felt like to sit cross-legged on the carpet or curled up on the couch, waiting. Because before streaming gave us everything all at once, we had to wait for our stories. And somehow, that made them even more worth it.

Television didn't just entertain us—it shaped us. It taught us about love and loss, friendship and failure, laughter and longing. It filled the silences of our homes and the spaces between our growing pains. The voices we heard through the speakers —funny, flawed, familiar—became the background music to our becoming. This section honours them. The shows that held us. The moments that stayed. The screen that lit the room long after we were supposed to be asleep.

TV Guide Tarot

She flipped past static, sitcoms and sermons, searching for signs in the reruns— wondering if fate came scheduled in half-hour blocks.

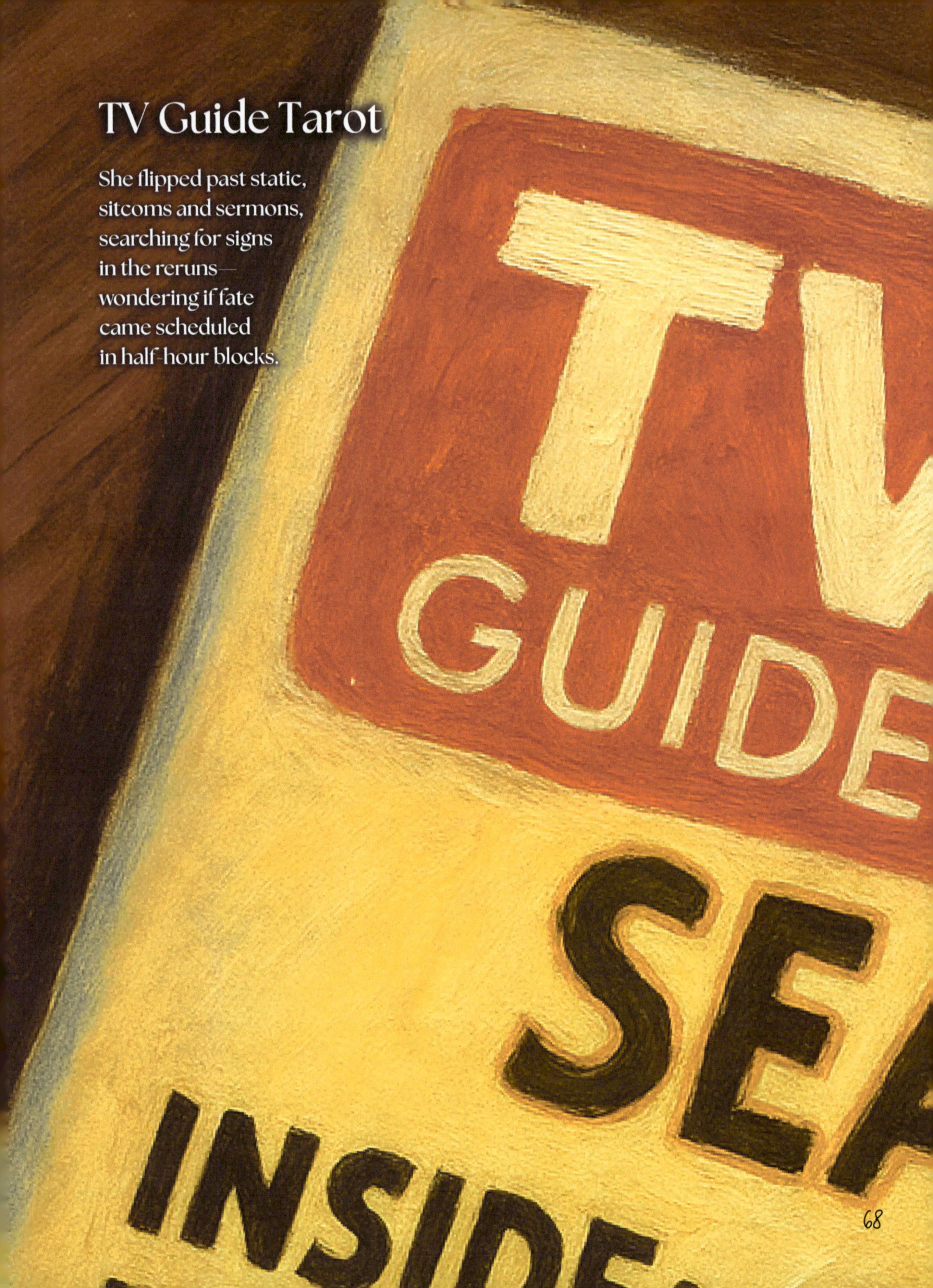

Saved by the Bell, Broken by the Rest

There was a time when everything could be fixed in twenty-two minutes.

A misunderstanding, a heartbreak, a math test failed and made up just in time. The world reset with every episode. Consequences were soft-edged. Lessons landed gently. You could count on laughter before the credits. You could count on the bell.

We watched it after school, sprawled on shag rugs or sun-warmed couches, a bowl of dry cereal balanced on our knees, the volume just loud enough to drown out whatever wasn't fair in the real world. There was something sacred about it. The way Zack always had a plan. The way Jessie always had something to say. The way everything always came back to friendship.

It didn't matter if we'd seen it before. That was the point. The rerun was safety. The predictability was a promise: no matter how messy things got, no matter how wild the scheme or how bad the outfit, it would all end with a smile. A joke. A freeze-frame that told us everything was okay.

Until it wasn't.

Until we grew up, and the bell stopped saving us.

The world started breaking in ways that couldn't be resolved before dinner. There were no laugh tracks to soften the blows, no school dances to make it better. Grief didn't show up in neon or scrunchies. It came quietly. It came in headlines. It came in real-time. And suddenly, innocence felt like something retro. Something grainy.

Something taped over and slowly wearing out.

Still, we go back to the reruns.

Still, we find ourselves mouthing the words before they're spoken.

Because some part of us lives there. Back in Bayside. Back in the simplicity of problems that could be solved with a pep talk or a timeout. Back when we thought a locker could hold the whole world.

We were saved by the bell once.

But we were broken by the rest.

This Is a Story All About How

This is a story all about how
a crown was worn sideways,
a boy became legend,
and a living room became a world.

We laughed—loud, often, together.
The kind of laugh that filled the space
between growing pains and growing up.
It wasn't just funny.
It was familiar.

Aunt Viv's side-eyes.
Uncle Phil's thunder.
Jazz, airborne again.
And Will—grinning, golden,
breaking the fourth wall like he was breaking the rules
just to reach us.

It was sitcom and sermon.
Gold chains and grief.
Fresh kicks and ancestral ache.
It never chose between comedy and truth—
it carried both in open palms
and offered them to us, gently.

And then—
the music slowed.
The room held its breath.
And a question, ragged with longing,
tore through the soft shell of the scene:
"How come he don't want me, man?"

We didn't know a show could do that.
Could know us like that.
Could touch the part of us
that we didn't show anyone—not even ourselves.

And somewhere in the middle of the ache,
we danced.

Because The Carlton—God bless it—
still might be the most iconic two-step of the decade.
Alfonso Ribeiro: a poet in pleated pants,
bending physics into punchlines,
moving like music had a secret just for him.
The most underrated comic genius of his time—
and he did it with his whole body.

This was a show that wore joy like armour
and sorrow like ceremony.
It gave us a seat on the couch
and a glimpse of ourselves.

This is a story all about how
we were raised by reruns,
taught by laughter,
broken open by one boy's question—
and pieced back together
by a family who wasn't ours,
but somehow always was.

Viewer Discretion Advised

The screen warned us.
Strong language. Violence. Mature themes.
But we stayed.
We watched the breakup. The betrayal. The beating. The death.
We watched the girl disappear and the boy not cry.
We watched a world we weren't old enough to enter,
and made room for it anyway.
We were kids.
But the warnings were never for us.
They were for the grown-ups who weren't paying attention.

The One Where They Were Everything

We thought adulthood would look like this—
a couch we didn't own,
coffee we couldn't afford,
six hearts orbiting a single orange frame.

They made thirty look like magic.
Like the rent was never due,
like heartbreak came with punchlines,
like no one ever truly left—not for long.

We watched them grow
in sitcom seasons and holiday episodes.
Through breakups and weddings,
through foosball and fridge notes,
through pivoting couches
and Chandler's awkward grace.

They were beautiful,
and messy,
and *ours*.

Rachel made mistakes in style.
Ross was an entire red flag in khakis.
Monica was control and care,
Joey was the softest soul in tight pants.
Phoebe was wild and wonder,
and Chandler—Chandler hid his hurt in the punchlines
and we loved him for it.

They were everything.

They were who we wanted to be
when we still thought adulthood meant
bagels, banter,
and someone always walking through the door.

Now we know—
life is lonelier than the laugh track let on.
Apartments aren't always filled with friends.
And couches don't hold entire worlds.

But they taught us how to be there.
How to grieve in the gaps.
How to come back from the things
we swore we couldn't survive.

In reruns, they're still waiting.
Still sitting at Central Perk,
still holding space for us—
like time never moved.
Like we never left.
Like we never had to grow up.

in syndication

same line.
same scene.
same silence where you wanted something different.

you watch it again anyway.
because it's yours.
and it always ends the same.

Sabrina Was My Religion

Sabrina was my religion.

Not because she was perfect—but because she was powerful.
Because she could freeze time with a finger snap and still forget her locker combination.
Because she made mistakes and magic in the same breath.
Because she was soft and strange and didn't always fit, and still—she mattered.
She was teenage and holy.
She was eyeliner and incantations.
She was awkward and adored.

I believed in her like other girls believed in boy bands.

And what a faith it was:
That your weirdness could be wonderful.
That your aunts could be your altar.
That your familiar could talk back and call you out.
That you didn't have to choose between love and ambition,
or between boy trouble and world-saving.

She wore her power like a cropped cardigan.
Sometimes too tight.
Sometimes slipping off the shoulder.
But always hers.

Sabrina taught me that girls could be chaos and light.
That we could hold the cosmos in our palms
while worrying about math class.

She wasn't a princess.
She didn't need rescuing.
She had a talking cat, a cosmic destiny,
and a moral centre that glittered even when the world went dark.

She was the altar I knelt before in my bedroom
with black eyeliner smudged under both eyes.
She was the reason I never once flinched when someone called me too much.

Because Sabrina taught me that too much girl
was exactly enough.

Code Blue at County General

It was always chaos.
Sliding doors. Screaming stretchers.
Gloved hands flying. Blood blooming in cotton.
A woman crying for her baby.
A man clutching his side like pain could be held still.
The whine of a monitor crashing into flatline.
The word *stat* like a prayer.

And beneath it all—
a pulse.
Fast, frantic, human.

ER didn't coddle us.
It handed us death in real time.
It taught us that sometimes you save the patient,
and sometimes you only save the moment.
Sometimes you lose the pulse.
Sometimes you lose the girl.
Sometimes you lose *yourself*.

We watched it like scripture.
Held our breath with the paddles.
Learned the language of grief in fifteen seasons.
We didn't need to know the medicine.
We knew the weight.

They were heroes, yes—
but broken ones.
Dr. Greene, gentle even when bleeding.
Carter, green then hardened.
Abby, all sharp edges and stitched-up hope.
And Luka, with a ghost in his throat
and a prayer in every silence.

They were exhausted and flawed
and impossible not to love.

We thought maybe we'd grow up to be that brave.
That scarred.
That *necessary*.

But *ER* wasn't just about doctors.
It was about the cost.
Of care. Of trying. Of showing up.

It was about what happens
when the hallway is too full,
when the light is too bright,
when the patient is too far gone
and you have to keep going anyway.

Time of death, 3:42 a.m.
And still, you scrub in for the next one.

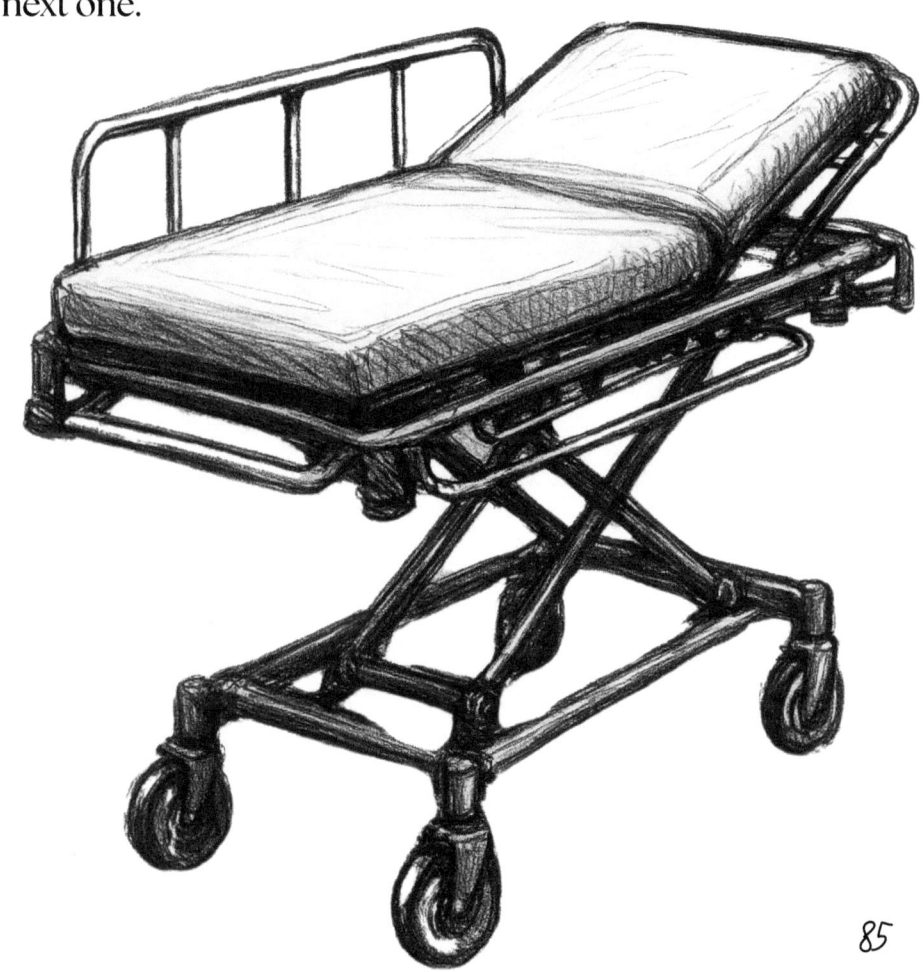

When Cory Loved Topanga

When Cory loved Topanga,
it was awkward and wide-eyed—
all cowlicks and locker doors,
the kind of love that didn't know how to sit still.

It started with crayons and weird haircuts,
with lunches traded and feelings unspoken,
a slow burn across school years
and three hundred episodes of almost.

He didn't always get it right.
He panicked. He flailed.
He talked too much.
He doubted what we were sure of.
And she—she stood still like a truth,
a knowing in a floral skirt,
too bright for the background,
too bold to be anything but seen.

Topanga was thunder in soft curls.
A girl who believed in destiny
even when the boy didn't.

They kissed in the rain.
They broke up in hallways.
They made up under applause.

They taught us that love could grow up with us.
That it didn't have to be perfect—
just present.
That sometimes the one who drives you crazy
is the one you can't walk away from.
That maybe fate is just a million tiny choices
to stay.

They made marriage look like the next step
after homeroom.
Like growing older together
could be as natural as reruns on a Friday night.

And maybe it was.
Maybe we believed in forever
because of how Cory looked at her
when he stopped trying to be funny.
Because of how Topanga said "yes"
with her whole chest
at the edge of adulthood
and never looked back.

They were clumsy.
They were corny.
They were everything.
And when Cory loved Topanga—
so did we.

SPECIAL PRESENTATION

The After School Specials

They aired after the bell.
Somewhere between cereal snacks and dinner.
Low-budget, heavy-handed,
shot in soft light and solemn piano chords.

They were the stories you weren't supposed to live,
but did anyway.

The girl who starved herself.
The boy who drank and drove.
The friends who let him.
The kid who smoked one joint
and ended up in prison, or worse.
The quiet one. The angry one. The girl with bruises
she said were from dance class.

We watched them with the lights still on
and our parents in the next room.
Like maybe if we paid close enough attention,
we wouldn't make the same mistakes.
Like shame could be an antidote.
Like fear could save us.

But we didn't just watch them.
We *took them in*.
Gulped them down like medicine.
We thought they were talking to us.
And maybe they were.

Because the lines blurred.
The locker rooms and living rooms looked familiar.
The pain felt close.
And the lessons—they stuck.

Not because the acting was good.
But because somewhere in the caution,
we saw a version of ourselves
that no one had warned us about.

They ended with freeze-frames and soft music,
but the ache lingered.
Like all the best stories do.

We don't talk about them now.
But some of us still live like there's a narrator
just off-screen,
waiting to remind us what not to become.

Black Box Glow

It waited for you.
Humming low.

Casting shadows across your face like secrets.
You told it everything
without saying a word—
just stared until it knew.
And it did.

Somehow, it always did.
The black box glowed,
and you felt less alone.
Even when it was just reruns
and the silence after commercials.

MuchMusic: Video Killed Nothing

We didn't just watch music.
We lived it.
Through a glass box in the living room,
or a fuzzy screen in the basement
where the VJs talked fast and the music was louder than the rules.

MuchMusic wasn't a channel.
It was a rite.
It was your crush in leather pants.
Your heartbreak on loop.
Your awkward adolescence lip-syncing into a hairbrush.

We counted down with it.
Top 30, top 10, all request, all chaos.
We discovered the bands that would become our beliefs.
Our friends.
Our lifelines.

There was something sacred about the way it knew us.
How it gave space for weird,
for loud,
for feeling everything at once.
You could laugh, cry, rage, and slow-dance
without ever changing the station.

We watched Much when we were too young to go out
but too old to feel nothing.
It filled the gaps.
Between school and sleep.
Between first kisses and final fights.
It made the noise bearable.

And when they said "video killed the radio star,"
they forgot to tell us that
videos also raised us.
Shaped us.
Saved us.

MuchMusic didn't kill anything.

It kept us alive.

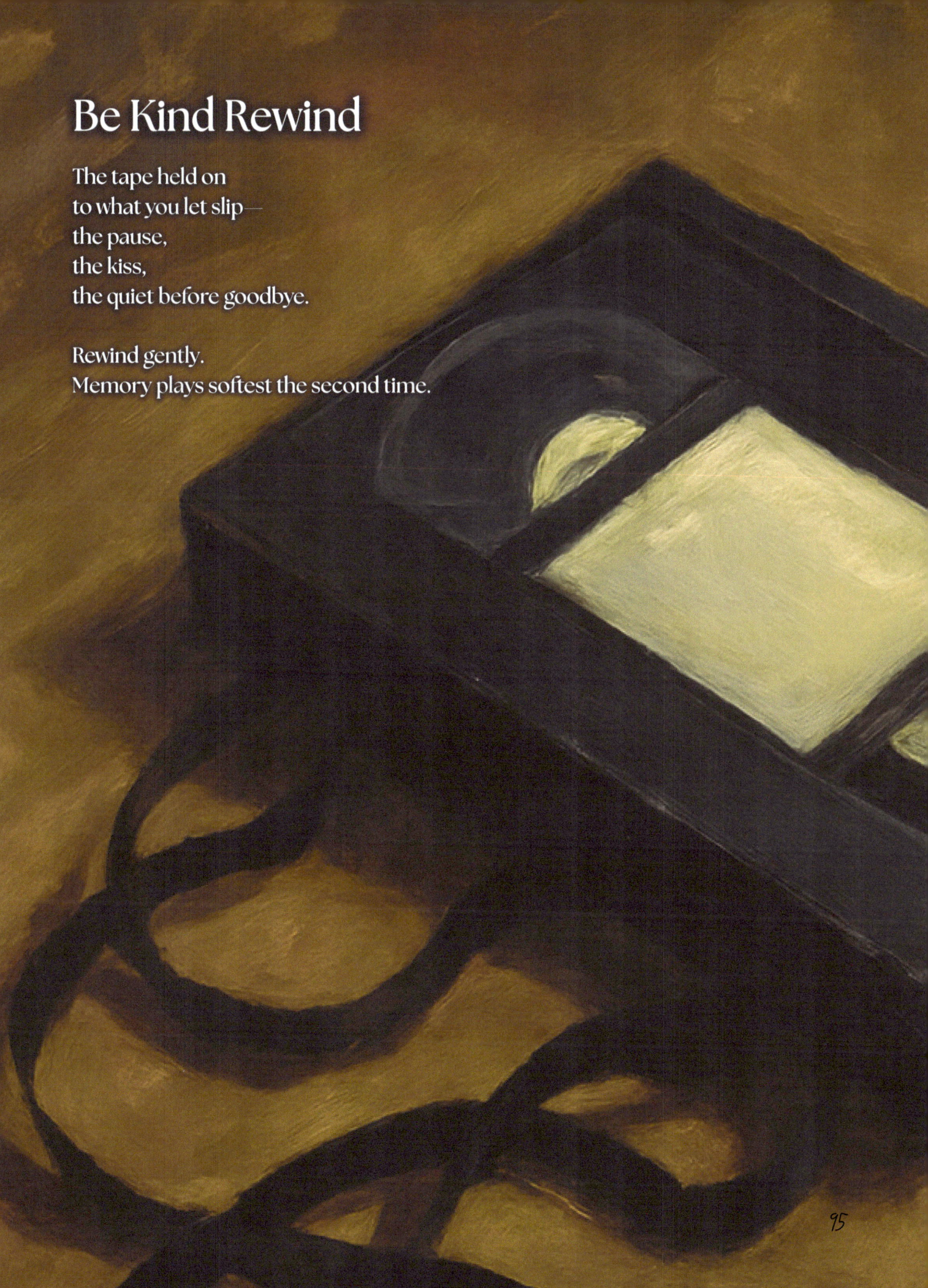

Be Kind Rewind

The tape held on
to what you let slip—
the pause,
the kiss,
the quiet before goodbye.

Rewind gently.
Memory plays softest the second time.

Wishing on a Dawson

You wanted to be loved
the way Dawson filmed things—
soft focus, perfect lighting,
every feeling a sweeping score.
But real heartbreak
never hits its mark.

They cried in metaphors.
Kissed like cliffhangers.
Made teenage pain
look noble.

And still—
we believed.

In Pacey's stammer.
Joey's impossible gaze.
A dock. A night sky.
A name whispered like regret.

We learned that soulmates
can show up too early
or too late.

Maybe that was the magic—
that nothing fit,
and we watched anyway.
Wishing it would.
Wishing on a Dawson
and calling it love.

X-Philes

Friday nights were for the unexplained.
For shadowed forests and cigarette smoke,
for Scully's doubt and Mulder's belief.
But more than that—
they were for me and dad.

We didn't talk much during the week.
He was tired. I was young.
But when The X-Files came on,
we met in the same room,
under the same flickering light,
and watched the world tilt sideways together.

I tried to stay awake.
Every week, I promised I would.
Sometimes I made it to the credits.
Sometimes only to the theme song.
But he never minded.
He never woke me.
He just let me sleep near him,
safe under a veil of aliens and questions.

It was more than a show.
It was a ritual.
The kind of sacred that doesn't need church.
Just a couch, a quiet understanding,
and the belief that the truth is out there—
somewhere between two people
willing to show up for each other
without ever needing to explain why.

We were X-Philes.
And I think, in his own way,
he believed in me
like Mulder believed in everything.

The VHS Tape We Wore Out

It was taped off TV—
Short Circuit 2,
with commercials paused
at just the right second
(or almost).

We wore out that tape
like it was sacred.
Because it was.
Not just for Johnny 5,
but for who we were
when we watched it.

All of us.
Together.
Before the quiet crept in.

We knew every line,
every glitch,
every moment the tracking fought
to hold on to the magic.

The laugh in the kitchen.
The pillows on the floor.
A closeness
you only understand
when it's gone.

A taped movie.
Paused commercials.
Popcorn.
A robot who just wanted
to be alive.

And we were.
Then.

Full House, TGIF

The laugh track never missed its cue.
The hug came right after the apology,
right before the credits.
And somehow, that was enough.

Friday nights were dipped in
saccharine,
packaged for safe consumption.
We were spoon-fed lessons
with piano music swelling underneath,
soft as a sigh and twice as practiced.

It wasn't real.
We knew it wasn't real.
But part of us still wanted it to be.

Danny's smile after a scolding.
Uncle Jesse's hair doing the emotional
heavy lifting.
A tidy moral tucked into every 22
minutes,
delivered like homework we didn't
mind doing.

Full House wasn't just a show—
it was the lullaby of a generation
trying to believe that problems
could be solved
before the final commercial break.

We were kids.
We believed a little too hard.
And maybe we still do.

Because there's something comforting
about a house always full.
Even if it's just light,
and music,
and make-believe.

Let Us Show You Something

It didn't knock.
It burst through the door—
brash, brilliant, unapologetic.
In Living Colour wasn't just a sketch show.
It was a seismic shift.
A dance break and a gut punch
delivered in the same beat.

They told the jokes nobody else would touch.
They danced harder, louder,
painted the world with neon truths
and let the punchlines fly.

The Wayans held the spotlight like it was overdue rent—
daring, dazzling, defiant.
Jim Carrey contorted himself into chaos on the side,
a wild card in a full deck.
And somehow, it all worked.

This wasn't your parents' comedy.
It was satire with swagger.
It was permission
to be loud, to laugh, to matter.

And in the flicker of the TV,
we saw ourselves
and everything we weren't supposed to say—
finally said.

So yeah,
let us show you something.
It might make you uncomfortable.
It might make you laugh so hard you
can't breathe.
It might just change what you think
comedy can do.
It did for us.

The Buffy Effect

She wasn't built to slay.
She was chosen.
Thrust into prophecy
like most girls are—
without asking.

The night became her inheritance.
A stake, her birthright.
Monsters in the graveyard,
monsters in the hallway,
monsters in her own chest.

She died.
She came back.
She kept coming back.
Because womanhood
is resurrection on loop.

It's fighting with mascara smudged.
It's grief and glitter,
bruised knuckles and open arms.
It's kissing the vampire
and still watching his hands.
It's knowing that softness
doesn't disqualify strength.

She was fierce—
and she loved anyway.
Loved deeply. Loved foolishly.
Loved like it wasn't dangerous.
And when love broke her,
she stood up
with every shattered piece
still glowing.

She made being strong
look like being real.

Every girl who watched
felt her spine harden—
then soften.
Felt seen. Felt sacred.
Not for what we survived,
but for how we stayed kind
in a world that kept
asking for our blood.

This wasn't just a show.
It was a spell.
A mirror. A battle cry.

We are the chosen.
We are the softness
and the steel.

We are
the Buffy effect.

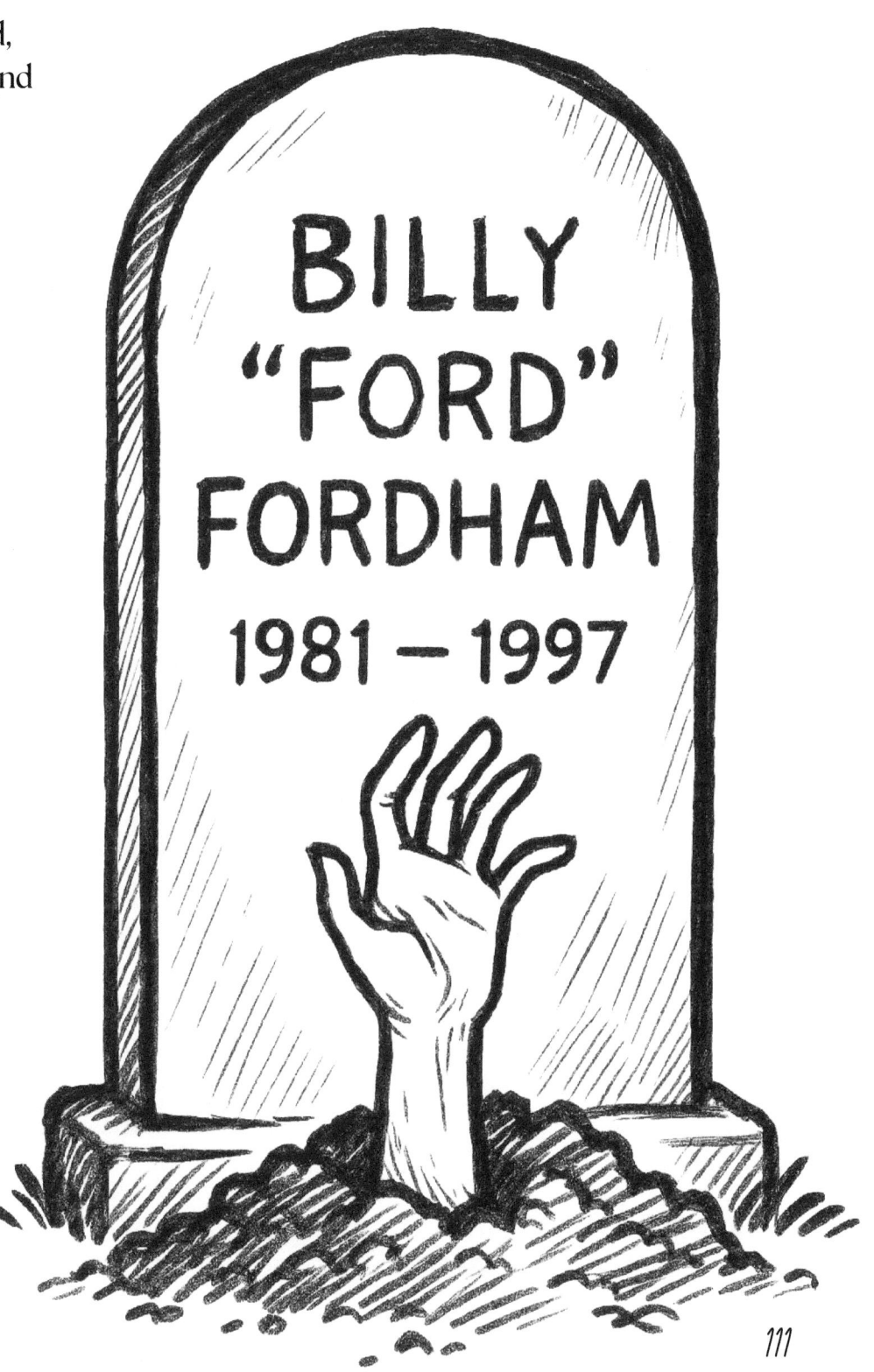

The Show About Nothing and So Much More

They called it a show about nothing, but that was never quite true. Sitcoms in the 90s weren't just thirty-minute slices of laughter. They were soft-glow mirrors, angled just so, reflecting an edited version of life back to us—funny, flawed, sometimes heartwarming, sometimes damaging, always familiar. In the era before binge culture, when we arranged our evenings around network schedules and held our breath through commercial breaks, these shows didn't just fill the silence. They shaped our expectations, rewrote our punchlines, and slipped their rhythm into the beat of our everyday lives.

There's comfort in the cadence of a sitcom. Conflict arises, hijinks ensue, someone storms out, the laugh track swells. And by the end of twenty-two minutes, there's a lesson tucked inside a joke. A problem solved. A hug shared. We were spoon-fed resolution, conditioned to believe life wrapped up neatly if you just held on through the ad break. For kids and teens especially, growing up in homes that weren't always warm or whole, this structure offered a kind of safety. It let us pretend that if we cracked the right joke or wore the right outfit or fell into the right friend group, everything would be okay.

In some ways, that mattered. Sitcoms gave us surrogate families—chaotic, messy, but always there in syndication. Full House told us that loss didn't mean the end of love. Family Matters showed that nerdy boys were worthy of their own space and spotlight. Boy Meets World taught a generation of kids that growing up was a slow, often ridiculous miracle. We saw best friends who never left. Parents who tried. Uncles who stepped in. Lessons softened with laughter, delivered like medicine in a spoonful of sugar.

And yet, for every lesson learned, a few were left unspoken. Or worse—delivered wrapped in stereotypes, sexism, or safe, shiny versions of the world that didn't always match reality.

For instance, the men. So many of them were, objectively, walking red flags. They were emotionally unavailable, immature, entitled, or downright cruel.

And still, they were the leads. They were the ones the beautiful, brilliant, overqualified women fell for again and again. George Costanza lies and manipulates his way through relationships and is never truly held accountable. Ross Geller is jealous, self-absorbed, and possessive—yet framed as romantic. Tim Taylor grunts his way through fatherhood, belittles his wife's opinions, and still ends up the hero. This wasn't just about the characters—it was about what those choices taught us.

The message came through clearly: mediocrity in men could be excused—even celebrated—if they were funny. If they were familiar. If they meant well. Meanwhile, women in sitcoms were expected to be patient, flawless, and funny without being threatening. They were allowed ambition, but only if it was cute. Allowed power, but only if it didn't scare the audience.

Sitcoms reinforced the idea that women had to make themselves smaller so men could grow—usually by the end of the episode.

Still, there were wins. We watched queer stories flicker into the mainstream, sometimes clumsily, sometimes quietly revolutionary. Ellen's "Yep, I'm gay" moment broke ground, even as the backlash nearly broke her career. Will & Grace tiptoed onto screens late in the decade, proving there was space—and demand—for more.

Representation was there, but rarely at the centre. Too often, it was the punchline. The sidekick. The sassy neighbour. The "very special episode." But we clung to those moments anyway. Because sometimes, crumbs were all we had.

What sitcoms did do brilliantly was give us cultural shorthand. We started speaking in references. Our friendships began to mimic the shows we loved—building tight-knit groups with overlapping storylines, casting ourselves as the sarcastic one, the neurotic one, the cool one, the heart. We longed for coffee shop booths and kitchen island heart-to-hearts. We believed that life would unfold in three acts, backed by a laugh track and resolved by bedtime.

Sitcoms also introduced us to nuance—albeit gently. They showed characters screw up and say sorry. They taught us to listen for subtext, to look beyond the joke. They eased us into topics like divorce, grief, poverty, and discrimination—always softened, always safe. But they gave us language. Sometimes, that's enough to start a bigger conversation.

And then there were the stings—the soft piano chords signalling that a lesson was coming. Cue the slow push-in, the meaningful glance, the moment when someone finally says the thing they've been holding in. It was manipulative, yes. It was emotionally engineered. But it worked. We needed it to work. For some of us, those moments were the first time we saw apologies modeled. The first time we heard the words, "I was wrong."

Was it enough? Of course not. But it mattered. And sometimes, it still does. Because even now, with thousands of options at our fingertips, we find ourselves crawling back to the familiar. We rewatch, not just for nostalgia, but for rhythm. For reassurance. For that strange, intimate magic sitcoms always held—the ability to convince us that the world might just make sense if we look at it sideways. That life, with all its mess and mediocrity, might still deliver something worth laughing at.

The sitcoms of the 90s were never just about nothing. They were about everything we didn't know how to say. They were stand-ins and safe places. They were cautionary tales and love letters, time capsules and escape routes. They shaped how we speak, how we flirt, how we parent. They helped us find our funny. And sometimes, our feelings.

They weren't perfect. But then again, neither were we.

And maybe that's why we loved them so much.

Late Night With Nobody

The hallway light hummed,
a pale substitute for company,
as the laugh track rolled in—
a chorus of strangers pretending not to be alone.

Syndicated friends,
worn like the sleeves of old pyjamas,
kept vigil with me
while the house exhaled in creaks and clock ticks.

A remote in one hand,
grief curled in the other,
I watched as time skipped
between commercials for car alarms and cologne.

Seinfeld re-runs taught me timing,
Frasier taught me wit,
Conan taught me to smile without meaning it—
and all of them taught me to stay awake.

Because sleep meant silence.
And silence was a mouth wide open
where memories echoed back,
sharp-edged and uninvited.

So I tuned in,
again and again,
to late night with nobody.
My favourite kind of nothing.

Tape Over

a birthday wish,
a laugh too loud,
a song we swore was ours—

taped over by a sitcom rerun,
lost beneath the hiss
of forgetting.

Britt's Fourth Birthday

Act III:
Hit Replay

Press Play to Feel Everything

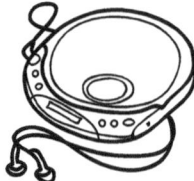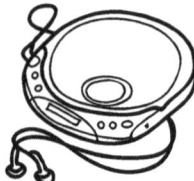

Music was the pulse beneath everything.

It thumped in our chests and buzzed in our headphones, spilled from our speakers and stitched itself into the seams of our teenage years. Before streaming, before skipping, before algorithms whispered what we should feel—we had burned CDs and bootleg mixtapes, songs taped off the radio with commercials still clinging to the intros. We played them on Walkmans and Discmans and that one stereo in the corner that always needed a thump on the side to work. We wore out the rewind button just to hear that one part again.

Every song was a lifeline. Every lyric, a secret scrawled in the margins of our notebooks. There was the angst of grunge and the ache of R&B, the sugar rush of bubblegum pop and the truth hidden in a sad girl's guitar. These weren't just background tracks—they were confessions and battle cries, dance floor anthems and rainy-day companions. We screamed them into the wind, sang them into our hairbrushes, let them say the things we didn't know how to say.

The 90s gave us a sound for every mood: the glittering highs, the devastating lows, the mess in between. We found ourselves in Nirvana's scream and Jewel's whisper. We raged with Alanis, slow danced with Boyz II Men, and healed with Lauryn Hill. We lived and loved and lost inside every chorus.

This section is a mixtape of memory. A rewind button pressed softly against the heart. These poems and prose are for the songs that got us through it—the heartbreaks, the house parties, the headphones-on-full-blast kind of days. They're for the melodies we still know by heart, the ones that play and suddenly we're back there, in the passenger seat with the window down, mouthing every word like a prayer.

Because music didn't just score our youth. It was our youth.

The Seattle Sound

It started with four open chords.
Unapologetically raw. Loud as hell.
Strummed with the indifference of someone who had nothing to prove
and everything to burn.

Then Dave Grohl hit the drums—
not like a metronome,
but like a fucking war cry.

And that was it.
That was the moment.
The before became the before.
The after became the after.

Grunge didn't knock.
It kicked the goddamn door in.

Smells Like Teen Spirit was more than a song.
It was the sound of a generation waking up,
shoulders hunched, eyes heavy, furious for reasons
they couldn't yet name.

MTV didn't know what to do with it.
Neither did radio.
This wasn't polished. It wasn't safe.
It didn't come with a smile or a love story.
It was sweat.
It was distortion.
It was truth.

The Seattle Sound wasn't born in a studio.
It was forged in garages, soaked in sweat,
wrapped in flannel, and steeped in sorrow.
It was everything mainstream tried to mute—
and it got loud anyway.

And then—this line:
"Our little group has always been and always will until the end."

Did Kurt know?
Did he feel the weight of those words
before they became legacy?
Before they became prophecy?
Before the end came too soon
and left us listening to echoes?

Nirvana didn't just shift the charts.
They split the timeline.
Before them: gloss, glitter, denial.
After them: truth, noise, pain—
and all of us finally hearing ourselves.

Change didn't whisper.
It screamed.
The Seattle Sound was here.
And nothing was ever the same again.

An Ode to the Rear

I like big poems and I cannot lie,
you other poets can't deny—
when a verse walks in with a rhyme-tight waist,
and a beat in your face—*you get sprung*!

Wanna pull up tough,
'cause this poem's got the stuff—
makes Shakespeare blush
and Emily clutch
her pearls with a proper "*Huff!*"

It's cheeky. It's loud. It's proud. It pops.
It doesn't belong in quiet workshops.
It belongs in jeans that can barely cope,
droppin' lines like a jump rope.

So if you're slingin' sonnets with a scowl and sneer,
just remember the wisdom of the lyricier:
You can keep your subtle little literary plot—
Me?

I'd rather rhyme like Sir Mix-a-Lot.

The Voice That Could Break a Century

It wasn't just a soundtrack.
It was a phenomenon.
The Bodyguard remains the best-selling movie soundtrack of all time—
not because of clever marketing
or blockbuster appeal,
but because Whitney Houston opened her mouth
and the world stood still.

When she sang, it wasn't performance.
It was transcendence.
She didn't need pyrotechnics or auto-tune or backup dancers.
She *was* the event.

And I Will Always Love You—
that impossibly soft opening,
that breathless pause,
and then that note—
it didn't just top charts.
It split time.
There was before Whitney sang that song,
and after.

She took Dolly Parton's gentle goodbye
and turned it into a cathedral.
She took pop ballads and made them operatic.
She took heartbreak and made it holy.

The rest of the soundtrack shimmered under her command—
I Have Nothing, Run to You, Queen of the Night—
each one a masterclass in power, control, and soul.
Even when she whispered,
she filled the room.

Whitney didn't just sing love songs.
She embodied longing.
She *was* the crescendo, the key change,
the stillness before the final note.

And yet, for all the talk of vocal range and technique,
what set her apart wasn't what she could do—
it was what she made you feel.

She made devastation sound like velvet.
She made euphoria sound like truth.
She made the impossible feel effortless.

We like to say voices like hers come once in a generation.
But the truth is—
they don't.
Whitney was singular.
Once ever.

The Bodyguard didn't just belong to the '90s.
It belonged to Whitney.
And Whitney belonged to something beyond all of us.

A gift too bright.
A flame too fierce.
And a voice we're still trying to live up to.

The Sign

It was on every mixtape.
Every car ride.
Every mall speaker near the food court.

I saw the sign—
and it opened up my dance moves.
My hips did that awkward '90s sway,
my hands did interpretive nonsense.
I lip-synced like my life depended on it.
(It didn't. But still.)

Was it deep?
No.
Was it everywhere?
Yes.
Did we love it?
Oh, absolutely.

We were not okay,
but Ace of Base made us bop
like we were.

Creep

It wasn't just a song.
It was a mirror.
Held up to every kid
who felt like too much,
or not enough,
or somehow both.

He sang,
and we flinched—
because it was ugly,
and honest,
and ours.

And for a moment,
being a weirdo
felt like a kind of power.

Truth-Tellers in Harmony

Before The Miseducation,
there were The Fugees—
a trio that turned hip hop into a force of elegance,
resistance,
and razor-sharp poetry.

They made sampling an art form,
made Bob Marley and Roberta Flack sound like prophecy,
and gave the world something it didn't even know it needed:
Lauryn Hill's voice.

She didn't just sing.
She testifed.
She rapped with a precision that silenced rooms.
She sang with a soul that cracked them wide open.
She stood beside men,
not behind them.
And she outshone them.
Effortlessly.

And then she went solo.
And The Miseducation of Lauryn Hill
didn't just arrive.
It *landed*—like gospel,
like revolution,
like someone had finally said out loud
everything a generation of women had been holding in.

Love, heartbreak, motherhood, faith, fury—
she put it all in there.
With no filter, no pretense, no apology.

She called out the world,
then turned around and called herself in.
She gave us Doo Wop (That Thing),
To Zion,
Ex-Factor,
and in doing so,
gave Black women space to be complicated.
To be divine.
To be whole.

Her only solo studio album.
And still—one of the most celebrated albums of all time.
Not because she disappeared after.
But because she *said everything she needed to say*.
Once.
Perfectly.

Lauryn Hill didn't give us a career.
She gave us a scripture.
And we're still studying it.

liner notes

in the margins,
beneath the lyrics,
tucked between
thank-yous and names
you'll never know—

are the feelings
too quiet
for the chorus.

the heartbreak
hid in fine print.

the truth
you only see
when you lean in.

Counting Crows
August and Everything After

The Most Flawless Album Ever Made (And I'll Die On This Hill)

August and Everything After doesn't begin. It unfolds. Slowly. Like grief. Like memory. Like the first breath you didn't know you were holding.

From the moment Round Here drifts in—half lullaby, half confession—you know this isn't just a record. It's a reckoning. Adam Duritz doesn't sing so much as bleed, and we followed his voice like a trail of breadcrumbs back to ourselves. These songs were for the lonely. The lost. The ones who never felt quite real until someone else told their story first.

This album isn't polished. It's raw in the way skin gets raw after too much crying, too much wanting. There's a rattle to it, a heartbeat. Every piano note is a shiver. Every lyric feels scribbled at midnight on the back of a receipt. Mr. Jones may have been the hit, but even it carries a desperate undercurrent: the longing to be seen, to be known, to be more than just a footnote in someone else's song.

And then comes Anna Begins. Oh god. Anna Begins. That's the one that levels you. Because it's not about love beginning—it's about the moment it ends and you're still pretending it hasn't. It's the softest heartbreak. The quietest goodbye. It doesn't scream. It accepts. But it's the kind of acceptance that tears you apart before it puts you back together.

Perfect Blue Buildings is a poem disguised as a song. Time and Time Again aches like trying to remember something you never fully knew. And Rain King? That's the scream into the wind, the declaration that pain and joy are made of the same notes, just played in a different key.

There is no filler here. No weak track. No break in the spell. This is not just music—it's narrative. It's longing. It's survival. August and Everything After was made for the over-feelers, the late-night thinkers, the ones who carry old wounds like souvenirs.

It's not about nostalgia. It's about truth.

And that truth is this: August and Everything After is flawless.

Not because it's perfect.

Because it's honest.

And that kind of honesty?

That kind never gets old.

"WELL, I DREAMT I SAW YOU WALKING UP A HILLSIDE IN THE SNOW CASTING SHADOWS ON THE WINTER SKY AS YOU STOOD THERE COUNTING CROWS"

When The Noise Fell Away

It begins with candles.
Flowers.
A stage dressed not like a concert hall,
but like a funeral.

And in a way, it was.

Nirvana: MTV Unplugged in New York aired on December 16, 1993—just four months before Kurt Cobain would take his own life. But no one watching that night, or in the years that followed, could shake the feeling that he already knew. There's a stillness to the performance, a spectral awareness, like the songs themselves were being played on borrowed time.

Stripped of distortion, stripped of volume, stripped of the armor that made grunge so powerful—Unplugged exposed what lay beneath Nirvana's chaos: vulnerability.

And it was devastating.

The setlist alone defied expectation. This wasn't a greatest hits parade. There was no Smells Like Teen Spirit, no Lithium. Instead, Kurt filled the hour with covers, obscurities, and deep cuts that read more like elegies than setlist choices. Songs like David Bowie's The Man Who Sold the World or Lead Belly's Where Did You Sleep Last Night weren't just performed—they were resurrected.

Cobain sang like someone already halfway gone.

What makes Unplugged so unforgettable isn't just what was played—
it's how it was played.

There's no screaming.
No smashing.
No sarcasm.

Instead, we get tremors.
We get cracks in the voice.
We get a man who seems to be singing directly to the void,
and finding, heartbreakingly,
that it sings back.

When All Apologies begins, it sounds like surrender.
When Something in the Way ends, it feels like confession.
But it's Where Did You Sleep Last Night that leaves a permanent scar.

By the final verse, Cobain's voice is less instrument than invocation—
rising, ragged, reaching for something just out of view.
His eyes flutter open at the end, wild and distant, like he's seeing something none of us can.

Then he looks down.
And it ends.

You don't need to know the headlines to feel the weight of that moment.
You just need to have ever lost something you couldn't name
until it was already gone.

In the mythology of Nirvana, Unplugged sits outside the frame.
It's not the sound of rebellion—it's the sound of reckoning.
For a band defined by noise,
this was silence weaponized.
This was grief before the grieving.

And maybe that's what makes it so hard to revisit—
not because of what happened after,
but because of what we hear now:
The exhaustion.
The beauty.
The humanity.

Nirvana: MTV Unplugged in New York isn't a concert.
It's a moment of clarity
before the storm finally wins.

It's the last breath before the plunge.

And all these years later,
it still feels like a secret
we were never meant to witness.

The Band That Took On the Giant

In the mid-90s, Pearl Jam did something few artists dared to do: they went to war with Ticketmaster.

At the height of their fame—when they could've just cashed in and coasted—they stood up for fans. Not their own egos. Not their profits. People. In 1994, the band filed a formal complaint with the U.S. Justice Department, accusing Ticketmaster of monopolistic practices and price gouging. At the time, Ticketmaster controlled the ticketing industry with an iron fist, adding outrageous surcharges that made concerts inaccessible for working-class fans. Pearl Jam, always grounded in their punk ethics and DIY spirit, called it what it was: greed.

They tried to organize a tour bypassing Ticketmaster venues altogether—choosing alternative locations, outdoor fairgrounds, and independent spaces. It was messy. It was complicated. It mostly failed. But it was never about winning.

It was about *trying*.

Pearl Jam's fight didn't dismantle Ticketmaster. But it did shine a spotlight on the corruption baked into the live music industry. It planted a seed of resistance. And in an era where corporations swallowed culture and artists stayed silent, Pearl Jam refused to play along.

They proved something bigger than ticket prices.

They proved integrity has a volume all its own.

Blue Smoke

It didn't shout.
It seeped.

Dummy played like a confession whispered
through a wall of static—
smoky, sultry, sad as hell.
It was noir for the broken-hearted,
trip-hop for the overthinkers,
a slow bleed of emotion
looped and layered
until you couldn't tell memory from melody.

Beth Gibbons didn't ask you to listen.
She made you ache.

That voice—
fragile one moment,
feral the next—
wrapped itself around your ribs
and stayed there,
like the echo of someone who left
without slamming the door.

Dummy wasn't built for the radio.
It was made for late nights,
bad decisions,
and the quiet sob
you swallow on the third glass of wine.

It was a mood.
A warning.
A world.

And once you entered it,
you didn't come back the same.

don't go chasing

waterfalls didn't ask for your attention—
it commanded it.
smooth harmonies carried hard truths
about grief, risk, and vanishing lives.

you sang along
before you realized it was a warning.
and maybe that's why it stuck.

because the truth,
when sung beautifully,
stays.

The Australian Invasion

Two voices.
Two sounds.
One country that quietly snuck into our ears
and never left.

Silverchair and Savage Garden couldn't have sounded more different—
but somehow, they both hit exactly when we needed them.

Silverchair was heavy.
Not just sonically—emotionally.
Daniel Johns didn't just pick up the torch Kurt Cobain left behind.
He cradled it.
He carried it like a burden,
writing lyrics that bled with anxiety, alienation,
and the disorientation of growing up under a microscope.

He was young—too young—
to be writing about pain so precisely.
But there it was: Freak, Tomorrow, Abuse Me, Ana's Song.
Songs that didn't sugarcoat the struggle.
Songs that made you feel seen,
even when you didn't want to be.
Silverchair gave voice to what so many were too afraid to say out loud.
They weren't just a grunge act from Australia.
They were proof that the ripple Kurt started
had reached the other side of the world—
and still hit like a wave.

And then—Savage Garden.

Suddenly, everything was bright again.
Romantic.
Sweeping.
Deliriously earnest.

Where Daniel Johns scratched at the walls,
Darren Hayes opened the windows.

Truly Madly Deeply wasn't just a song.
It was a vow.
A wedding staple.
A promise whispered under disco lights
and backyard fairy lights alike.

There was To the Moon and Back,
I Knew I Loved You,
Affirmation—
songs that dared to be dreamy
at a time when cynicism ruled.

And wasn't that brave, too?

Because vulnerability takes many forms—
one screams into the void,
and one sings softly
while holding out its hand.

Silverchair and Savage Garden.
Grit and gloss.
Roar and reverie.
Two acts from Australia who reminded us
that emotion, in all its volume and texture,
deserves a stage.

And honestly—
whether you were headbanging in your bedroom
or slow dancing in a high school gym,
you had them both on your mixtape.
Right where they belonged.

The Angry Young Women

That's what they called them.
As if that was a flaw.
As if anger wasn't sacred.
As if it wasn't earned.

Alanis Morissette. Fiona Apple. Meredith Brooks. Paula Cole. Liz Phair.
They weren't angry *instead* of being talented.
They were angry *because* they were paying attention.

And holy hell, were they talented.

They didn't just write songs.
They wrote manifestos.
They turned heartbreak into rebellion.
They turned shame into gospel.
They screamed when we weren't allowed to.
They whispered when we weren't supposed to.
They showed their teeth and didn't apologise.
They bled onto the mic and dared you to look away.

These women wrote about things girls were never supposed to feel.
Rage. Lust. Disappointment. Disgust.
They named the things we were told to swallow
and sang them so loud,
we finally started spitting them out.

And still—
they were mocked.
Dismissed.
Called too emotional. Too dramatic. Too much.

Too angry.

Because women, we've learned,
aren't allowed to feel too much of anything.
Smile, and we're vapid.
Cry, and we're hysterical.
Yell, and we're insane.
Feel nothing, and we're cold.
Feel *everything*, and we're dangerous.

But the angry young women—
they didn't care.

Or maybe they did,
but they said it anyway.
They told the truth.
And the truth made people uncomfortable.
Especially the ones who were used to hearing women
sing only about love
and not the way it gutted them.

You Oughta Know was a detonation.
Criminal was a confession with a serrated edge.
Bitch was an anthem, not an apology.
Where Have All the Cowboys Gone?
wasn't really a question—
it was an indictment.
And Fuck and Run was a revelation
before we even had language for hookup culture
or internalized shame.

They cracked something open in us.
And we haven't closed it since.

Call them angry.
Call them messy.
Call them dangerous.

But never forget—
they showed us it was possible
to tell the truth,
and still take up space.

They weren't angry instead of being brilliant.
They were brilliant because they refused
to stay silent.

Woman Behind the Feedback

She wanted a band.

Not a scandal, not a headline, not the mythology we stuffed her into. Just a band. Just the music. Just a place to scream into the mic loud enough to wake the dead—and maybe herself along with them.

Courtney Love loved harder, louder, and messier than the world was ready for. She loved music the way some people love oxygen. She loved Billy. She loved Kurt. And she was punished for all of it.

Where men were allowed to rage and self-destruct with impunity, she was dissected. Where male musicians were celebrated for their rawness, she was dragged for hers. When she screamed, it was "unhinged." When she roared, it was "hysterical." When she dared to front a rock band, it was "manufactured." And when she excelled—when she dropped Pretty on the Inside like a blood-stained glove across the face of the early '90s, when she followed it with Live Through This, a record that still splits the sky in two—we took it away from her. We handed the credit to the men.

To Kurt. To Billy. To anyone but the woman who actually wrote the songs. You can't search Courtney's name without stumbling over some half-baked theory about how Kurt wrote the whole record. You can't read a review without being reminded of her proximity to men the press deemed more talented, more tragic, more pure.

As though she didn't have her own hurricane to summon.
As though her lyrics didn't scrape the underside of girlhood, addiction, fame, and fury with a surgeon's hand and a scream that could rattle your ribs.

Courtney rocked harder than most men ever dared. She ripped herself open onstage and gave us the messy truth when polished lies were easier to sell. And for that—we crucified her.

But here's the thing: Courtney Love never needed your permission.

She only ever needed a band.

And goddamn, she had one.

The Flowers Were Dead

Dolores didn't ask you to feel.
She *dragged* you into it.
That voice—
equal parts lullaby and battlefield—
didn't just sing grief.
It *sounded* like it.
It cracked through the speakers
like a mother wailing at a funeral
only she showed up to.

No Need to Argue was not a breakup album.
It was a reckoning.
A dirge for peace.
A love letter to the disillusioned.
It carried the weight of colonized blood,
of sons turned to soldiers,
of girls made small for loving too hard.

It was Ireland, and every bruised country.
It was a woman's roar,
draped in a Sunday dress
with combat boots beneath.

The flowers weren't just dead.
They had been laid at the feet
of something holy and ruined.

And Dolores sang like she had seen
every god we believed in
walk away.

parklife vs. champagne supernova

london laughed in technicolour,
cheeky and sharp—
a pint, a pun,
a shrug at the sky.

manchester dreamed in grayscale,
eyes cast upward—
a prayer, a plea,
a hymn made of haze.

one talked.
one ached.
and the rest of us
chose a side
by how we felt
at sunset.

When the World Needed Glitter and Grit

We were eleven
or thirteen
or somewhere in between
learning how to take up space
with bubble letters
and bare midriffs
and friendship like warpaint.

They arrived loud—
platform shoes slamming
onto a stage that hadn't made room
but was about to anyway.

We didn't have the words for it yet—
this strange, sudden ache
to be more than pretty.
To be Scary.
To be Sporty.
To be Posh or Baby or Ginger.
To be *chosen*.
To be *many things at once*.

And there they were,
like neon prophecies—
telling us what we wanted,
what we really really wanted,
was to never again be small.

We learned choreography like gospel,
sang with hearts cracked open
and hairbrush microphones.
We called each other by names
we'd pulled from CD inserts
and claimed our personas
like saints or spells.

They weren't perfect.
Neither were we.
But they showed us how
to shout instead of whisper,
to dance even when they told us to sit still,
to chase dreams with glitter on our faces
and gum in our mouths.

Girl power wasn't cute.
It was *radical.*
It was five women,
and then millions,
rewriting the rules
in Union Jack sequins
and unapologetic noise.

They left, eventually—
as all lightning bolts do.
But they lit the path.
And some of us never turned back.

like thunder

he hit like thunder and smiled like summer.

every beat he dropped rewrote the rules—
louder, faster, fuller.

you didn't just hear dave grohl.
you felt him.

Two Voices, One Legacy: Reflecting on 2Pac and The Notorious B.I.G.

There are names that feel like echoes of an entire generation. Tupac Shakur. Christopher Wallace. 2Pac. Biggie. Pac and Big. Their names weren't just names. They were shorthand for something larger than music, something heavier than fame. They were the soundtrack of a decade, the voice of a people, and the pain of a fractured mirror we've still never managed to piece back together.

To talk about 2Pac and Biggie is to walk a tightrope of reverence and reality. It's too easy to turn their story into folklore. Too tempting to flatten them into symbols. But they were people. Complicated. Brilliant. Flawed. Human. And maybe that's where we need to begin—not with their rivalry, but with their humanity.

Tupac was fire—pure, raw, unpredictable. He could deliver fury and softness in the same breath, often did, and often left us wondering which side of him would show up next. He wasn't just a rapper. He was a poet, an actor, a philosopher, and at times, a prophet. His music carried the pulse of protest and the ache of vulnerability. You could feel his heartbreak in "Keep Ya Head Up," his rage in "Hit 'Em Up," his reflection in "So Many Tears." There was always more than one layer. Always more than one version of the man.

Biggie was the counterweight. Where Pac was sharp edges and storm clouds, Big was smooth lines and low thunder. His flow was effortless—liquid and heavy, like molasses dripping from gold. There was something hypnotic in the way he told stories, something that made even the darkest realities sound cinematic. "Juicy" is joy and longing. "Suicidal Thoughts" is a scream inside a whisper. He made his pain palatable, even beautiful. He made us listen.

Together, they redefined hip-hop. Not just as a genre, but as an art form, a cultural force, a reflection of lives that had gone ignored for too long. They raised the stakes. They widened the lens. And tragically, they became casualties of the very system they helped expose.

The East Coast–West Coast rivalry has been dissected to death—reduced to headlines, memes, and arguments that miss the point. This wasn't about coasts. This wasn't even about Pac and Big, not really. It was about the pressure cooker that fame creates when it sits on top of trauma, pride, and unresolved grief. It was about how young men—brilliant young men—get caught in currents too big to swim out of. And how often, when power is watching from the shore, nobody throws them a line.

It's easy to forget how young they were. Pac was 25. Big was 24. These weren't elder statesmen of the culture. They were barely out of boyhood. And yet we handed them the mic and the mantle, the weight of representation, the burden of being more than just artists. They carried it as best they could. Until they couldn't.

And yet, somehow, they're still here. Not physically, of course, but here—in samples and murals, in verses quoted like scripture, in the way a crowd still roars when the opening bars of "California Love" or "Hypnotize" hit. Their music hasn't faded. If anything, it's grown louder, clearer, more urgent. We return to it not just for nostalgia, but for clarity. For connection.

Because the truth is, we needed them. We still need them.

They gave us more than music. They gave us permission. To speak. To rage. To question. To feel. They reminded us that joy and grief can live in the same line, that masculinity can hold softness, that survival is its own kind of poetry. They showed us that art isn't supposed to be clean or easy. It's supposed to cut.

Today, we remember them not as martyrs or myths, but as men. As brothers, sons, artists. As human beings who lit up the sky while they were here and left us with a fire we're still trying to keep lit.

There's no neat ending to their story. No moral. No resolution. Just the music. Just the memory. Just the ache of what could've been.

But maybe that's enough. Maybe that's everything.

the first song i ever cried to

not the whole song.
just one verse—
quiet, buried,
a line no one else seemed to flinch at.

but it landed like a secret
i didn't know i'd been keeping.

"you're just like an angel / your skin makes me cry"
— and i did.

because it was too much
and not enough
and exactly
how i felt.

Ahead by a Century: For The Tragically Hip

They weren't just a band.
They were the breath between winters. The blood between generations.
They were Canada's quiet heartbeat—the one we didn't notice until it stopped.

The Tragically Hip were with us, always.
In backseats and barbecues. On dock wood still warm from the sun.
In corner store parking lots with Slurpee-stained tongues and nowhere to be.
In school gymnasiums where we slow-danced to lyrics we didn't understand yet,
but *felt* anyway.

They lived in our bones.

Gord sang like he was pulling the earth up through his ribs.
Like he could taste every war, every love, every loss this country had ever held.
He didn't just tell stories—he carried them.
Wore them like wet denim.
Turned them into elegies and shouted them into the wind
so we could hear what it meant to be here.
Really here.

In all our broken, frozen, sprawling, aching glory.

We didn't need the world to understand them.
They were ours.
Unpolished. Unapologetic. Undeniably us.
The sound of small towns and sleepless nights.
The poetry of the overlooked.
The holiness of hockey tape and highway signs
and knowing that even the most average lives
can carry the most extraordinary truths.

And maybe we didn't always listen closely—
until that final tour,
when he stood on stage
fragile and ferocious,
giving us everything he had left.
Like a prophet.
Like a storm.
Like a man who knew how much he mattered
and gave us one last chance to say thank you.

Thank you, Gord.
Thank you, boys.
Thank you for the soundtrack of our survival.
For reminding us that no dress rehearsal means we'd better feel this life,
even the hard parts.
Especially the hard parts.

Because loving something doesn't mean it lasts forever.
But if it sings loud enough—
if it tells the truth–
it echoes.

And The Hip?
They'll never stop echoing.

Not here.

Not now.

Not ever.

Lilith Fair

It wasn't just a concert.
It was a *gathering*.

A communion of women and girls and mothers and friends, in sandals and sundresses, in Doc Martens and flannel. Some of us came crying. Some came angry. Some just wanted to *feel* something that didn't come from the radio stations run by men who always played the same five bands.

And then we saw her—Sarah McLachlan, backlit and barefoot, holding her guitar like it was the softest thing she owned. She didn't yell. She didn't need to. Her voice was a balm and a reckoning. She sang like she'd been listening to us the whole time.

Lilith Fair wasn't loud like the others.
It was *open*.

It made space for sorrow. For storytelling. For sitting with our own feelings without rushing to erase them. Tracy Chapman singing truths that hushed an entire field. Fiona Apple tearing herself wide open onstage and handing the wound to us. Shawn Colvin, Emmylou Harris, Paula Cole, Joan Osborne—each of them different, each of them necessary. And then there were the lesser-known names, the ones we scribbled down in the backs of our journals so we wouldn't forget. The ones who would score our quietest years.

It was the first time some of us heard lyrics that felt like our lives.
Like someone had finally written down what it meant to be overlooked, to be underestimated, to be tired and still full of fire.

There were no costume changes.
No backup dancers.
Just women and their instruments.
Just feelings, thick in the heat.

And we stood there, shoulder to shoulder, girls and women and grandmothers, singing along like it mattered. Like it would echo somewhere. Like it would make the world softer, or at least more *aware*.

Lilith Fair told us that our voices had value.
Not because they sounded sweet,
but because they *sounded real*.
And that was enough.

The Blueprint was Missy

Before we had a word for it—
for being loud and weird and brilliant
and *fine with it*—
we had Missy.

She didn't knock on the door of hip-hop.
She built her own, shaped like a spaceship,
and walked through it like it had always been hers.

Missy Elliott didn't just bend genres.
She bent time.
She blurred the edges of what a woman could be
in rap,
in R&B,
in music at all.
She danced in garbage bags,
spit bars that made you grin and rewind,
and carved out a space so original,
so unapologetically *her*,
that no one's ever managed to copy it—
though god knows, they've tried.

She made beats feel like body rolls.
Verses like bounce houses.
Hooks like trap doors.
She wrote for everyone—
your favourite artist's favourite song
probably has her fingerprints on it—
and yet, when she stepped to the mic herself,
it was like hearing the future
in real time.

There was no blueprint for Missy.
So she became one.

And through it all—
the hits, the history, the heat—
she never gave up being weird.
Never gave up being *funny*.
Never gave up being *herself*.
And maybe that's the most revolutionary part.

Missy didn't fit into the mold.
She melted it.
And turned it into a beat.

napster

we stole everything—
like tiny, denim-clad pirates with dial-up.
called it freedom.
called it love.
called it *just one song*.

it was magic.
it was chaos.
it was theft.

and yeah—
we knew.

White Boy Ragecore

It wasn't just music.
It was a *temper tantrum with a soundtrack.*
Limp Bizkit. Papa Roach. Korn. Staind.
Dudes in JNCO jeans, barking into microphones
about how misunderstood they were—
by their dads,
by their girlfriends,
by society,
by *everyone*.

It was suburban angst with a seven-string guitar.
It was locker room trauma wrapped in distortion.
It was red fitted caps and black nail polish
and *a lot* of yelling.

And somehow, it worked.
It gave voice to a very specific kind of fury—
not revolutionary,
not righteous,
just *loud*.

The genre was called nu-metal,
but let's be honest:
it was *White Boy Ragecore*.
And it peaked at the exact moment
we were all getting broadband
and energy drinks.

These weren't protest songs.
They were grievance anthems.
Less "fight the system,"
more "you can't tell me what to do, Mom."

But—
and here's the thing—
we still screamed them in our cars.
We still jumped around at house parties.
We still found catharsis
in the absurdity of it all.

Because sometimes,
the world doesn't need poetry.
It needs a grown man screaming about his stepdad
over a crunchy riff
and a DJ scratching for reasons unknown.

It was angry.
It was messy.
It was mostly dudes.

And yeah—
it probably should've come with a warning label
and a therapist's business card.

But for a while,
White Boy Ragecore was the sound
of a generation trying to feel big
in a world that made them feel small.

And now,
we listen back
with one part cringe,
one part nostalgia,
and the quiet relief
that we made it through that phase alive.

Woodstock '99

By the summer of 1999, the world was crackling with pre-millennial tension—Y2K panic, corporate domination, boy bands, and dial-up fatigue. The internet was waking up. Columbine was still fresh. Rage was currency, and music was loud about it.

So when Woodstock was resurrected once again,
people wanted to believe.

They wanted to believe in the original spirit—of peace, love, and music.
Of messy, muddy, magical rebellion.
But what they got in Woodstock '99 wasn't a revival.
It was a reversal.
Of ideals.
Of hope.
Of what music could be.

Held on a decommissioned air base in Rome, New York—more concrete than grass, more fencing than freedom—Woodstock '99 felt less like a festival and more like containment. A marketing scheme dressed up as nostalgia.

Everything cost something.
Bottled water? $4.
Shade? Good luck.
Security? Overwhelmed.
Accountability? Nonexistent.

And the *music*—the very thing that was supposed to unite people—did the opposite.

The setlist leaned hard into the fury.
Korn. Limp Bizkit. Rage Against the Machine. Metallica.
It was curated testosterone.
A soundtrack for catharsis, yes—
but without any of the soul or spirit
that defined the original Woodstock thirty years earlier.

By the time Fred Durst screamed "Break Stuff,"
the crowd had already started to believe him.

They broke things.
They burned things.
And far, far worse,
they broke people.

The Time of Your Life

it wasn't a punk song.
it was the breath between chords—
a hush in the riot,
a parting glance in a room still echoing.

not a scream,
but a whispered middle finger
tucked inside a thank-you.

you played it at graduations,
at funerals,
as summer slipped from your hands—
anywhere a goodbye wore soft shoes
and didn't make a scene.

it never claimed
this was the time of your life.
it only hoped,
in its small, quiet way,
that it meant something.

and now,
so do we.

Rewinding Softly

We didn't know we were building something we'd carry forever.

Not in the quiet way the VCR hummed before the tape clicked into place. Not in the way the dial-up tone pierced the room like a call to something bigger, stranger, more infinite. Not in the smell of a Blockbuster on Friday night, or the way our fingers hovered over "record" during our favourite song on the radio—hoping the DJ wouldn't talk through the intro.

We were just living it. Wearing butterfly clips and baggy jeans. Burning CDs for people we loved. Falling in love with fictional characters and learning how to fall in love with ourselves. We weren't taking notes. We didn't know it would all vanish so quietly.

But that's the thing about growing up—you never really notice when it's happening. Not until years later, when a song comes on in a grocery store and suddenly you're seventeen again. Heart cracked wide open. Whole world still waiting. Every feeling turned up so loud you could barely hear yourself think.

This anthology wasn't meant to be a eulogy. It's not a scrapbook or a playlist or a punchline. It's a *rewind*.

Back to a time that didn't try so hard to brand itself.
Back to cluttered bedrooms and slow dances.
Back to real-time goodbyes and in-person hellos.
Back to the weird, wonderful, awkward in-between of figuring it all out.

We didn't know we'd miss it.
But we do.

Because it never really left, did it?
It lingers—in our rhythm, our references, our reverence. In the way we still talk about mixtapes and teen dramas and the songs that meant something. It's in our bones now, humming beneath the surface. Not just the music, but the moment. The moment we became.

So, if you're here at the end—thank you.
Thank you for remembering with me.
Thank you for feeling it all again.
Thank you for pressing play, one more time.

Now hit rewind.

Softly.
Lovingly.
Like it mattered.

Because it did.
And it always will.

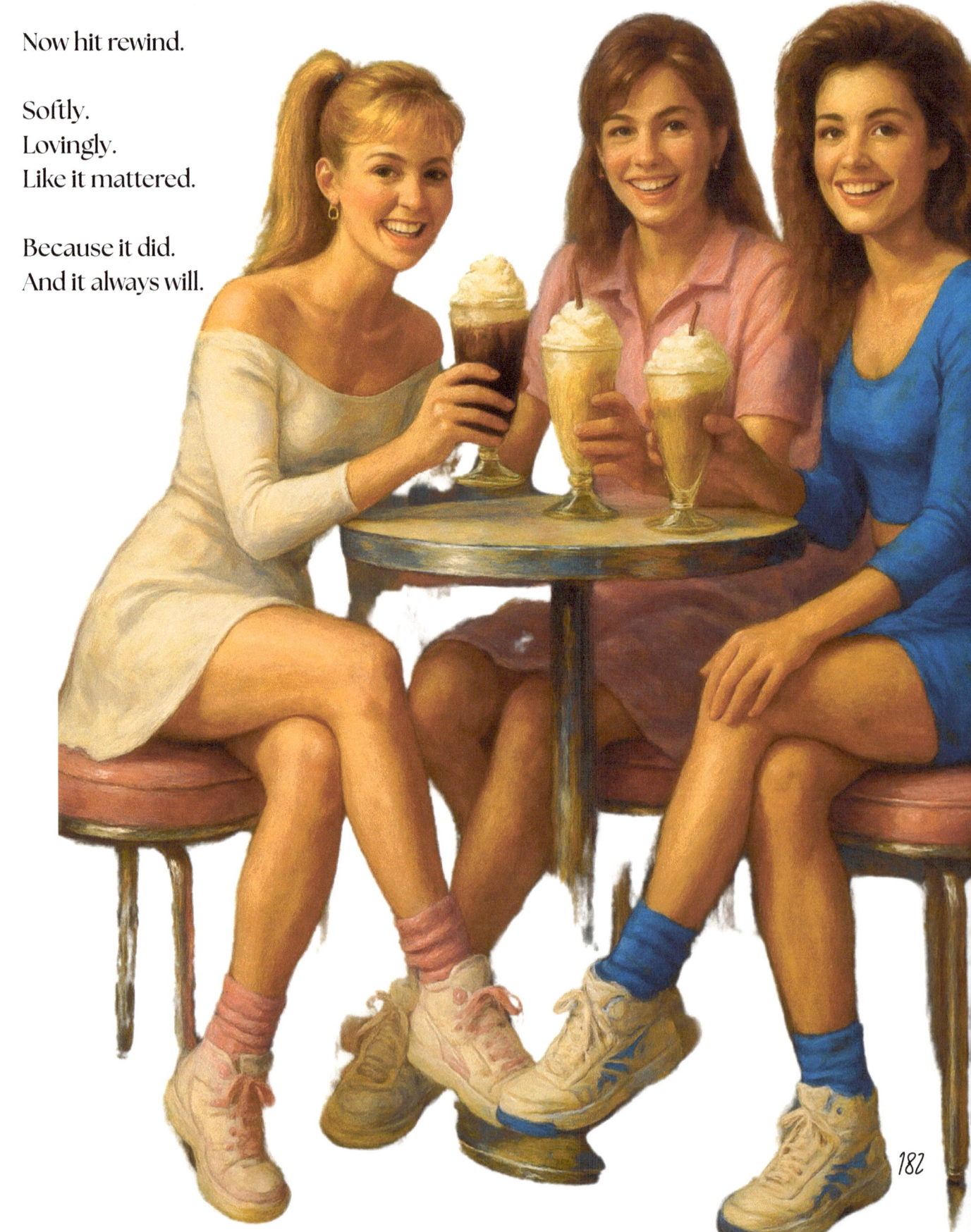

183

The Pages Between us: Poetry and Prose Anthology Series

Poetry and Prose is more than a series.

It's a heartbeat.

It's an evolving collection of themed anthologies, it blends the sharp clarity of prose with the lyrical pull of poetry—because some things can only be said when form dissolves, and truth rushes in.

Each volume stands on its own. A singular expression. A capsule of time and feeling. But together, they hold a mirror. To what we remember. To who we've been. To what it means to be a person walking around with a soft heart in a hard world.

Inside these pages, you'll find emotional truth, cultural fingerprints, and the tender, unflinching edges of being human. From the rage that builds in silence to the softness that survives it. From the echoes of first love to the questions that haunt our becoming. From nostalgia to reckoning.

Each anthology is an offering.

Each one asks only that you feel.

Dial-Up and Daydreams is Volume I of the Poetry and Prose series—a love letter to the 90s and the kids who grew up there. It captures a decade of awkward transitions, pop culture awakenings, and the aching beauty of adolescence in a world that was slower, louder, and often wonderfully unfiltered. This book is your mixtape, your yearbook, your sleepover confessional. It's the start of something that already lives in your bones.

About The Author: Britt Wolfe

Britt Wolfe is a 90s girl, through and through. Raised on MuchMusic countdowns, mix CDs made with real intention, and the kind of sleepovers where you stayed up talking about everything and nothing until the sun came up. She learned early that words had weight—and she's been trying to catch them and pin them to paper ever since.

Now grown (technically) and based in Calgary, Alberta, Britt is a writer, creator, and daydreamer who still wears her heart on her flannel sleeve. She's the kind of woman who believes in the magic of slow dances, the healing power of a good cry in the car, and the fact that the right lyrics at the right time can change everything. She writes with tenderness and truth, laced with dry wit and the emotional fingerprints of someone who felt everything deeply and kept going anyway.

Britt is also the founder of Just Cat Things and the creator behind the Songs To Stories novella series—stories inspired by the music that shaped a generation. Whether she's building something tangible or something fictional, Britt shows up with grit, grace, and an undeniable spark.

She lives with her wildly supportive Australian husband, their sometimes-possessed cat, Lena, and Sophie—the best husky in the entire world. Her work is a love letter to growing up, to surviving it, and to the stubborn hope that we never stop becoming.

brittwolfe.author@gmail.com

brittWolfeAuthor

@the.banality.of.britt

BrittWolfe.com